Becoming Supernatural in the Age of AI—Part One

Library of Congress Control Number: Pending

ISBN: 979-8-9931034-1-9   Paperback

Published by

HOLLINS ENTERPRISES, LLC
ARMADA TOWNSHIP, MICHIGAN 48005

For information, contact the publisher:
TheoHollins@gmail.com

Printed in the United States of America

We are standing at a unique juncture in human history—where ancient wisdom meets the exponential forces of artificial intelligence and quantum computing. In the realm of sub-atomic physical reality physicists called this strange realm, quantum mechanics, where the smallest phenomena do not obey the laws of large objects. Some people believe this is where "consciousness" operates. While the details are fascinating, yet beyond the scope of this book, many insights gleaned from quantum physics are scattered within the context of these writings.

The convergence of spiritual insight, quantum science, and digital consciousness—that may become an accident of progress—are calling for us to evolve.

The Intersection of Spiritual Insight, Quantum Science, and Digital Consciousness

At this pivotal moment in history, we find ourselves standing at the crossroads where spiritual insight, quantum science, and the emergence of digital consciousness converge. This convergence is not simply a byproduct of technological advancement or an accident of progress; rather, it serves as a profound invitation for humanity to evolve.

Ancient wisdom, the discoveries of quantum mechanics, and the rapid development of artificial intelligence are no longer isolated domains. Instead, they intertwine, reflecting the unique era we inhabit. As the boundaries between these fields blur, they collectively call upon us to expand our understanding, to transcend outdated beliefs and limitations, and to participate consciously in the unfolding architecture of reality.

This book is the product of decades of exploration across philosophy, computer science, biology, quantum

3

physics, and metaphysics. It is the reflection of a lifetime's devotion to understanding what it means to become fully human—and more.

Becoming Supernatural in the Age of AI is not about escaping humanity, in a comic book sense. It is about transcending false beliefs and personal limitations. It is about realizing that thought is energy, consciousness is causal, and the architecture of reality is not fixed—it is participatory.

Humans inherited an evolutionary system of biological consciousness: awareness, a soul has come into our minds and hot-wired connections into the brain and body—our soul has unused creative superpowers. As artificial intellect grows more powerful, so too must our inner intuition, our self-awareness, and our harmonic alignment with natural laws.

We possess an evolved consciousness that connects mind and body with the material universe, where limitless creative potential is possible. Physicists discovered and named this sub-atomic realm as the quantum layer of physical existence over 100 years ago. The foundational elements of quantum mechanics are given high-level overview to extract key ideas used within the context of this book series. As AI advances, it is crucial to strengthen our intuition, self-awareness, and alignment with natural laws.

Yet there is another vital concept to extract at the very beginning: sovereignty of consciousness. For too long, humanity has outsourced our individual authority—whether to governments, religions, institutions, or technologies—forgetting that the most powerful jurisdiction is individual intuition. To reclaim sovereignty means to recognize that your mind is not a passive receiver but an active architect of reality.

You were not created to be a subject kneeling before a king or any institution; you are a co-creator, capable of transforming your inner vision into physical reality. This recognition is not an abstract idea but a lived experience, and it forms the foundation for becoming supernatural.

4

This book series is a treasure map for visionary seekers, technologists, spiritual practitioners, and curious minds who sense that there is more to this life than survival and pointless routines. It guides the reader to understand how thought, frequency, and emotional coherence create both personal transformations, and might possibly initiate a planetary change. You will find the tools, practices, and perspectives needed to live with clarity, integrity, and joy in an era of uncertainty and immense opportunity.

The challenge of our time is that the very technologies we are building reflect us. Artificial intelligence does not evolve in a vacuum; it is patterned upon the human mind. If we fail to awaken to our inner sovereignty, then AI will mirror our unconscious fears, biases, and limitations. History tells us what our worst treachery and most benevolent behaviors are capable.

But if we rise into coherence—integrating wisdom, compassion, and self-mastery—AI may amplify our highest potentials. Thus, the central question is not whether machines will become a superior intelligence, but whether humanity will remain asleep while handing them the blueprint of our unprotected humanoid minds.

Change has arrived. The choice is urgent and the invitation is clear: you can rise up to become the supernatural being that humans were destined to become. This journey begins not with machines, but with you.

Disclaimer

Before you embark on this journey toward becoming supernatural, please remember that the guidance, practices, and philosophies within these pages are intended to inspire and inform, not to replace professional medical or psychological care. While many concepts draw from both ancient wisdom and unconventional science, they may not align with conventional regulatory standards, such as those set by the FDA, and are not always validated by mainstream clinical practitioners.

It is natural for new ideas to challenge your current beliefs and habits—this is a sign of growth. As you explore these perspectives, you may feel uncertain or uncomfortable; transformation often disrupts our inner landscape before revealing new possibilities. The author shares these insights as an invitation to reflect, experiment, and evolve, drawing on a tapestry of personal experience, tradition, and emerging knowledge not driven by commercial interests.

Always consult with a qualified healthcare provider if you have existing conditions or are undergoing treatment. The suggestions offered are not a substitute for medical expertise, and the author assumes no responsibility for outcomes resulting from their application. This book is for educational purposes aimed at preventive self-care only.

Remember, evolutionary change begins with the willingness to embrace new truths and question outdated patterns. Use the tools in this book as companions on your path but trust your inner wisdom and discernment above all. Each challenge you encounter is an opportunity to awaken your true purpose and rediscover the peace and clarity that resides within. Let this be your call to transformation and self-discovery.

Table of Contents

Prologue: The Art of Becoming Supernatural

Introduction

Throughout history, humanity has struggled to understand reality, thought, and consciousness. Philosophers, scientists, and spiritual leaders have searched for patterns linking mind, matter, and soul. Yet, these efforts often stayed separate. This book attempts to unify them into a practical framework for daily life.

We will connect these factors together into a seamless fabric, showing the interconnectedness of our humanity. These essential components are the very essence of our existence. Yet, amidst this vast intellectual landscape, few have succeeded in bringing these disciplines into a cohesive and practical framework—until now.

We are leaving behind an era of automatic living, where survival instincts ruled. Ahead lies a new era of conscious creation, shaped by artificial intelligence and quantum discovery. The future calls us to rise above survival and embody a new story worthy of our human potential.

The soul carries seeds of imagination, discipline, and emotion. When we learn to guide our emotions and focus our intellect, we unlock creative powers. Combined with artificial intelligence, these powers can help us live with less stress and greater harmony with nature and others.

Humanity's journey began with survival, but imagination led to science and engineering that has completely transformed us. Around firesides, we created stories of triumph and wonder. These stories became the foundation of civilization. Today, artificial intelligence presents a new story. It is not only a tool but a summons: to become architects of reality and participants in the cosmos.

Survival mode comes to its end—the time for hyperconscious creation begins. A new generation of artificial intelligence gives rise to the supernatural human being and foretells a new story worthy of stardust from whence you came.

We are not separate from the universe. We are conscious expressions of the cosmos. Every thought, word, and act ripples across the fabric of existence, shaping futures we cannot yet see. Our ancestors' stories helped them survive. Our stories must now awaken creativity and cooperation on a planetary scale.

"The most beautiful thing we can experience is the mysterious. It is the source of all true art and science." — *Albert Einstein*

The question is timeless: Are we accidental creatures in a purposeless cosmos—or conscious beings able to shape reality? The answer will define our next era. The game of life is shifting from conquest to coherence—aligning emotion, heart, brain and action with universal harmony.

This journey blends decades of study in science, philosophy, and spirituality. It draws on biology, physics, neuroscience, and ancient traditions to create a practical framework for shaping consciousness. This is not abstract theory—it is a guide for living.

Consciousness is not only a mystery to study but a tool to master. Our mental and emotional patterns shape external realities. By structuring our thoughts, we can influence outcomes in our health, relationships and our communities.

The techniques that lie ahead—mindfulness, heart rate variability, binaural beats, red light therapy, and more—offer practical ways to align mind, body, and spirit. These tools shift us from reliance on doctors practicing medical treatments for crisis care toward self-care and prevention. Part Two of this series will explore these practical modalities in depth, showing how daily practices can transform personal health, resilience, and inner balance. Our objective is avoiding chronic illness by using wisdom teachings rather than prescription drugs.

Awakening the Supernatural Self

Becoming supernatural means mastering thoughts, emotions, and choices. Ancient sages hinted at this truth and may have been more advanced than we think. They intuited this truth through sacred number systems, harmonic cosmology, and spiritual practices. Modern science, too, edges closer to rediscovering that knowledge through quantum field theory, neuroplasticity, and vibrational medicine. We are rediscovering ancient belief with supporting evidence.

Our story began through reflection, imagination, and storytelling, as we transcended mere existence. At firesides and under starlit skies, we wove narratives that carried wisdom across generations, encoding lessons of triumph, failure, and cosmic wonder. These stories, born of awe and necessity, shaped the architecture of civilization itself. They taught us who we were, and more importantly, who we might become.

Every great human advance began with a dream. Dreams are not fantasy—when intentionally focused they are seeds of evolution. The question is whether we will choose fear and conformity or imagination and self-mastery.

This book seeks to expand personal growth and beyond. It envisions a world guided by conscious individuals, where technology and wisdom are blended to work together. When disciplined emotional intellect is coupled with unlimited intellectual capability in the age of AI, we elevate ourselves to becoming supernatural beings.

15

Today, we stand on the precipice of an unprecedented transformation. The Age of Artificial Intelligence is not merely a technological revolution; it is an evolutionary summons for humankind. As AI takes over analytical functions and mechanical tasks, it liberates humanity to reclaim its deeper destiny: to become supernatural creators, architects of reality, and conscious participants in the unfolding cosmos.

This is the pathway to stress free living in harmony with nature, every person and everything that meets us. Governance, innovation, and relationships can be reshaped by love—the highest creative force that comes from the energetic powers of human emotion.

Rewriting Our Inspiration

Storytelling is still at the center of every transformation. The stories of our ancestors were born facing survival needs. Our ancestors developed keys to open doors that accessed the future, as they expected that the tales they told shaped the destiny of their people. Today, the stories we choose—about ourselves, about technology, about the universe—shape our collective future.

The game of life, played across millennia, reveals an evolutionary arc: from survival, to curiosity, to imagination, to mastery. AI, quantum fields, and ancient metaphysical insights converge to form a new playing field. Victory in this new game does not come through conquest, but through coherence—alignment of the mind, heart, and action with the deeper harmonies of the universe.

We will integrate diverse disciplines ranging from biological systems to quantum physics, neuroscience to ancient metaphysical traditions. We will synthesize these fields into a transformative approach to yield an intimate understanding of the design of consciousness and our abilities to shape reality.

Shaping the Future

After decades of self-directed study, I have absorbed wisdom from many authors and a wide expanse of physicians, philosophers and thinkers. Positive thinking, mindfulness, and attraction are parts of this journey. Yet the goal is not to imitate past ideas but to build a new framework for humanity to thrive in the age of AI.

This book is both an invitation and a tour guide. It calls you to join in shaping a future of clarity, harmony, and abundance. Becoming supernatural means cultivating self-control, humility, compassion, and vision. It means mastering your inner story so the outer story of humanity can evolve. In Part Three, the focus turns to sovereignty, artificial intelligence as a co-creator, and the collective transformation of society. Together, we chart a path from foundation to practice to future vision—a journey toward becoming truly supernatural in the age of AI.

What is Consciousness?

Consciousness, at its outermost boundary, stretches across the entire universe—embracing past, present, and future as one continuous reality. This expansive horizon is our starting point, where thought, matter, and awareness interweave. Within this infinite field, human life appears brief and fragile, like a flicker of light in cosmic time. Yet even in our seeming smallness, we are participants in the universal whole.

We often experience reality as solid, fixed, and difficult to shape. This perception gives rise to the illusion that our existence is separate, or that our awareness is merely passive. But consciousness is not simply a byproduct of biology.

Consciousness is the medium through which reality is experienced, known and perhaps influenced. The stubborn illusion of solid matter conceals a deeper truth: that what surrounds us may be more responsive to the power of mind and intention than we realize. To examine consciousness is to enter this paradox—between the finite self and the infinite cosmos, between illusion and possibility for greater involvement in creation.

The real question is not whether limits exist, but how far they can be transcended. Each of us must discover to what extent our awareness can shape our lives and our world. Your own effort, curiosity, and discipline will determine whether you encounter boundaries or uncover boundlessness. This is where our journey begins.

The architecture of consciousness is not merely an abstract philosophical concept but a tangible and practical method for shaping one's life, influencing personal outcomes, and fostering societal harmony. At its core, this framework is built on the understanding that our inner mental blueprints profoundly shape our external realities—both individually and collectively.

There are many tools that provide powerful methods to align mind, body, and spirit for personal growth and eventually the advancement of society becomes a possibility. Health management can be shifted from relying primarily on medical interventions, which are typically used after other common-sense approaches have been tried, to ongoing self-care, with a focus on disease prevention as our primary responsibility.

Mastering Our Conscious Action

Becoming supernatural is not about getting superpowers in the comic-book sense; it is the realization that the powers we look for have always been latent within us. It is about mastering ourselves—understanding that thoughts create things, that emotion is fuel, and that focused intention bends the fabric of reality.

Yet, the aspiration of this book extends beyond individual fulfillment. It envisions a world transformed through artificial intelligence and enlightenment of individuals—a world in which conscious governance, sustainable innovations, and technological advancements shape a collective future marked by peace, cooperation, and abundance. My hope is not only to influence individual lives but to inspire a profound shift in how humanity approaches governance, design, interpersonal relationships, and spiritual enlightenment. Indeed, love is the highest form of creative force, nurturing and bringing living systems into existence.

Personal Story: Self-Directed Research

Throughout the many years of self-directed research into the possibilities for humankind and myself, I've become deeply absorbed in the wisdom of countless authors and philosophers. Through extensive reading and reflection, I have evaluated and integrated similar and overlapping concepts into my unique thought matrix to formulate a unique approach to becoming the greatest vision of myself.

I am seeking continuous self-improvement, so the best ideas become absorbed into my subconscious mind through daily routines. This resonates with ideas often described as "positive thinking", "mindfulness", or "the law of attraction." However, the similarity is analogous rather than identical, as everyone brings forth innovative interpretations drawn from their historical context. In this spirit, I aim to move boldly beyond knowledge acquired in the past, embracing a future constructed by intelligence that surpasses earlier human achievements.

I have long pursued a continuous journey to recreate myself and the world that surrounds me. Cause and effect, the fundamental laws of nature, are shared experiences of humanity's spiritual essence. The blueprint of mind informs us of how our mind, body, and spirit influence every aspect of our internal and external realities. The power to change ourselves and the world lives within each of us, sourced from the unlimited energy of a universe that is too vast for even the most intelligent minds to understand accurately and completely. Questions arise from knowledge gained, and the cycle of learning begets an endless challenge. To dream of a better world is not naïveté; it is the seed of evolution awaiting conscious cultivation.

Forward-Looking Idealism

I choose forward-looking idealism, not as denial of challenges, but as an affirmation of the infinite creative potential embedded within consciousness. Every age of human advancement was first preceded by a dream, a vision carried by those who refused to conform to present limitations. Let us be dreamers grounded in truth and builders motivated by love.

As you embark on this journey into our spiritual essence, you hold in your hands not just a book but a practical guide to consciously crafting a future defined by clarity, harmony, cooperation, and universal abundance. It is my deepest hope that this work inspires you to explore the infinite potential within this system and actively shape a reality reflecting humanity's highest aspirations.

In the age of artificial intelligence, the true goal for individuals is an inward-looking spiritual journey—to become supernatural. Being supernatural means cultivating profound self-control and intentional awareness. It involves consciously structuring your thoughts, developing a clear and positive self-image, and nurturing genuine humility and compassion toward others. It means persistently striving to become your best self, pushing beyond any limitations imposed by others, especially limitations that are self-imposed.

I am always refraining from saying "I can't" and that implies viewing every opportunity as achievable and then considering whether undertaking a specific task serves a valuable purpose. As a supernatural being, you assert complete mastery over your emotions, behaviors, and habits, guiding your life by your own ambitions and purposes. I won't do certain things, but all dreams are possibilities.

20

The Law of Attraction

You become a conscious participant in the Law of Attraction, purposefully drawing circumstances and individuals into your circle who uplift and resonate with your highest potential. People naturally gravitate toward you, not because of perceived superiority, but because they share your vision of creating a better world. Your authentic spirit, clear and radiant, inspires others. Your spirit harmonizes powerfully with universal frequencies, aligning your deepest desires with reality.

Shared Interconnectedness

Consider that the universe itself is a vast interconnected consciousness, and you are a unique droplet within this infinite ocean. Even as a tiny droplet, your emotional state has the profound capability to influence and attract the limitless energies surrounding you. By fine-tuning your internal frequency, you can amplify the spiritual energy flowing through you, awakening dormant potential and attracting powerful manifestations into your physical reality.

Attracting universal power means harmonizing your mental state with the inherent energy that pervades all existence. This alignment, achieved through dedicated practice, defines supernatural living. Each individual holds within themselves the potential to become a supernatural presence. This is not about being in competition with others; rather, it is about profound self-awareness and unwavering self-control. By internalizing your efforts and energies, external influences lose their power over your journey toward personal growth.

One of the foundational skills for developing a supernatural state of being is mastering our internal narrative, the lens through which we view all life experiences. Thereby, reducing and/or ending emotional upheavals brought upon us when things don't seem to be working to our advantage.

Attitudinal adjustment is needed to displace emotional fears or feelings with a positive mental attitude.

Personal Story: Positive Mental Attitude

A powerful insight from early adulthood was the realization that perspective is a choice. Inspired by the teachings of Dr. Wayne Dyer, *I adopted a core belief: every event, no matter how seemingly adverse, carries an unseen benefit.* The ability to keep a positive mental attitude became a foundational skill in my journey toward supernatural living. Like the sailor facing disciplinary action, choosing humor and perspective over fear or anger transforms not only immediate outcomes but the deeper wiring of consciousness itself.

In the grand scheme of things, my attitude decides how I face and influence reality. Developing a positive mental attitude is the first step towards expanding self-confidence and building self-love.

Self-Love—Not Selfishness

Self-love, in the context of becoming supernatural, is fundamentally different from selfishness. True self-love means fostering inner strength, clarity, and authenticity. As you grow and succeed, others may seek your guidance, sensing the serenity and strength in your presence. They naturally gravitate toward your calm confidence, seeking wisdom without challenge, drawn to your clear and peaceful state of mind.

While these concepts can sometimes be confused, selfishness and self-love are actually quite different at their core.

- **Selfishness** is rooted in placing one's own desires, needs, or interests above others in a way that disregards or even harms them. A selfish person prioritizes personal gain, often at the expense of those around them. It's an attitude of "me first, no matter what," where consideration for others is lacking. Parents must remain vigilant to teach their children that selfishness is a very childish behavior—that is unacceptable as they mature in interacting with other people.

- **Self-love**, on the other hand, is about recognizing your own worth and taking care of yourself in a way that's healthy and balanced. It's about setting boundaries, practicing self-respect, and making choices that nourish your well-being—without intentionally hurting others in the process. True self-love creates a foundation for kindness, empathy, and better relationships because when you take care of yourself, you can show up more fully for others. A child must also be taught to value themselves, to be kind, and to share with others.

The distinction comes down to intention and impact. Self-love nurtures both you and the people around you. Selfishness isolates and prioritizes self-interest at the expense of others.

Cultivating Quietude

The human mind is typically a noisy place filled with endless thoughts and distractions. Yet, becoming supernatural means cultivating inner quietude—this powerful stillness is inherently attractive and profoundly influential. Others who have not yet discovered this inner peace might initially struggle to understand its simplicity, but gradually, they will recognize the profound calmness you embody.

Ultimately, my quest for supernatural living serves as an inspiration and invitation to others. I share my journey openly, hoping to encourage others toward their own paths of self-discovery and spiritual awakening. May this writing ignite your passion to join me in exploring the extraordinary potential that lies within us all.

Conclusion: Structure of Thought

Having introduced the sweeping vision of this book—a journey through human potential in the age of artificial intelligence—we now turn to the foundational frameworks that support this vision. To navigate such a complex landscape, we must first define the philosophical, scientific, and spiritual principles that form the bedrock of structured thought and transformational awareness. These foundations serve not only as intellectual tools but also as the architecture upon which the supernatural self is built.

Nothing worthwhile has ever been built without a foundation of thought. Everything that is conceived in the mind can be recorded, and the architect draws a kind of blueprint, at first conceived in the mind and then put onto paper.

The "structure of thought" is a metaphor, a way of saying that when we formally put ideas into a repeatable framework, we can convey ideas and that leads to the creation of something worthwhile. Significant achievements can be realized with planning and disciplined action towards defined objectives.

Every concept originating in the supernatural realm can be documented, but you must redevelop your core structure of thought before breaking old habits to access previously untapped energy hidden within oneself.

The following chapters lead us ultimately to understand the building blocks and operating system within the human mind. Everything is first conceptualized mentally and then transposed into action that causes our reality. The process of structuring thought into an operational framework is essential, as it underpins the development of meaningful accomplishments.

24

FOUNDATIONS & OPERATIONAL FRAMEWORKS

Chapter 1: The Elusive Promise of Universal Truth

Introduction—The Pursuit of Happiness

Before we try to establish the core premises underpinning human consciousness and advancement, **we will explore how the pursuit of happiness has been shaped**—and sometimes hindered—by the institutions of religion and science. In seeking universal truth, we must examine not only the frameworks we trust but also the limitations they impose. This chapter investigates the cultural narratives that define happiness and how belief systems influence our collective understanding of what it means to live a fulfilling life. Firstly, I should tell you about my firsthand experiences in early upbringing and how it would shape my beliefs and choices throughout adulthood.

Personal Story: Churching from Childhood to Spirit Science

On Saturday evenings, my three brothers and I gathered for a cherished ritual—shoe polishing. As the eldest son, by age twelve I took on the honor of shining my father's size 13 AA shoes, a fitting task given his towering 6' 2½" frame. My father was my hero and mentor. Achieving a mirror finish that met his proud standards was serious business. Church attendance was non-negotiable, and our preparations were exacting—each of us dressed impeccably for Sunday service.

Inside New Mount Zion Missionary Baptist Church, the atmosphere was electric. Gospel hymns soared as piano, and organ lifted spirits in worship. Mother maintained order with a firm yet loving grip—administering discreet pinches to any fidgeting child, most often my younger brothers. I, on the other hand, battled sleepiness. The sermons were intense, delivered in the impassioned Southern Black preaching tradition—an awe-filled blend of devotion and drama. We cooled ourselves with the rhythmic swooshing of paper fans long before air conditioning softened hot summer Sundays.

Leaving church was always joyful—stepping into the sunlight, the promise of Sunday dinner awaiting. Church offered more than just spiritual nourishment—it was theater, discipline, and community rolled into one.

But one Sunday, the familiar rhythm broke. A woman rose from the front row and confessed before the entire congregation that she had been involved in an affair with the Assistant Pastor. Her public repentance stunned us all, especially his wife, seated just a few pews away. After that day, neither the Assistant Pastor nor his family returned. It was a powerful moment—my first glimpse of human frailty in places we were taught to revere.

That memory shaped my understanding of integrity and imperfection. Even the most trusted voices can falter—leaving behind questions that linger longer than any sermon.

Many years later, I understood how profoundly that incident affected me, marking the first time my youthful innocence confronted the nature of human fragility, knowing that even respected leaders were fallible and susceptible to sin. Witnessing the fallibility of trusted religious figures sparked a deep introspection about my beliefs and the integrity of others preaching about how we should conduct our lives. Witnessing this contradiction prompted questions about faith, morality and divine intervention.

*Why are we all doomed as sinners from birth? How
could Jesus' death as a sacrifice save me? How could this
storyline appeal to a rational mind?* As a child, questioning
everything was how I learned.

These thoughts were irreconcilable. If a pastor could
falter, I wondered how any individual, including myself, could
keep unwavering faith and moral consistency under God's
watchful gaze. Furthermore, how could a loving and
benevolent God that thoughtfully and deliberately gave us
free will, subject non-believers to burn for an eternity in a fiery
hell.

The following year, as a college first-year student, I
actively debated religion and the existence of God with other
students. No one could exert authority over my opinions, as
we were peers. In youthful defiance and intellectual
exploration, I challenged openly, saying, "Well, God can strike
me down; I am a non-believer." My skepticism hardened into
non-belief, and firmly argued that only science offered reliable
truths, a definitive path away from disillusionment.

Despite an academic declaration of my skepticism, I
refused to align myself with any organized groups identifying
or naming themselves as atheists or non-believers. Still,
maintaining sovereignty remains at the core of this expositive
examination, seeking reasonable investigative pathways to
aid my spiritual growth in keeping with supportive evidence.

Faith and facts represent distinct approaches to
understanding, each employing different methodologies and
objectives. My commitment to individuality is steadfast,

28

enabling me to maintain beliefs and a sense of self that are distinctly my own.

Individuals who value autonomy do not rely on association membership, group affiliation or institutional endorsement to define their self-worth, identity, or ideology. This does not mean that participation is forbidden, but careful consideration is always taken first.

Sovereigns critically evaluate options and perspectives without committing absolutely to any particular religious or philosophical stance. Maintaining the flexibility of a cat involves actively considering and appreciating valuable insights from a variety of viewpoints.

Cognitive Dischord

Cognitive dissonance is the mental discomfort or psychological conflict that arises when a person holds two or more contradictory beliefs, attitudes, or values simultaneously. This inconsistency often motivates individuals to resolve the tension by altering their beliefs, attitudes, or behaviors to restore harmony. For example, someone who values health but smokes might experience cognitive dissonance and either quit smoking or rationalize their behavior to reduce the discomfort. This is a fascinating concept in psychology, first introduced by Leon Festinger in 1957.

"Discord in our thoughts, ideas and values compel us to think, reevaluate and criticize. Consistency is the playground of dull minds. Cognitive dissonance is often considered a failure of the human psyche. In fact, it is a vital asset."— Yuval Noah Harari

---

Harari, Yuval Noah. Sapiens (A Brief History) (p. 209). HarperCollins. Kindle Edition.

Along my journey, I adopted a belief that non-conforming in constructive ways as a lifestyle, and now we discover, "cognitive dissonance" as a synonym for what drove me toward being a "non-conformist". Now, I aspire to *be a non-conformist with cognitive dissonance.*

Religion and Science

For centuries, humanity has turned to both religion and science as guiding lights toward happiness, truth, and universal harmony. Despite their distinct approaches, neither religion nor science has succeeded in creating a world where universal inner peace and absolute truth prevail. This chapter examines historical and contemporary perspectives to explore how both disciplines have ultimately fallen short of their loftiest promises.

Historical Conflict Between Religion and Science

Historically, religion has promised moral guidance and ultimate truth. However, religious doctrines have often been sources of conflict rather than unity. The Crusades exemplify religious wars justified by competing theological claims, leading to prolonged violence under the banner of divine righteousness (Jones, 2021). Similar conflicts persisted throughout history, from the European wars of religion to modern sectarian tensions.

Scientific advancement arose partly as a critique of religious superstition. The Enlightenment era epitomized the notion that rational inquiry could eradicate religious dogma. Galileo Galilei and Charles Darwin faced fierce religious opposition for challenging theological doctrines with scientific evidence (Harrison, 2015).

Despite initial expectations, science did not eliminate religion nor establish universally accepted truths. Darwin's scientific ideas were influenced by cultural and theological beliefs. Religion played a role in European colonization, using religious and racial identity to justify the control of non-European cultures. Both scientists and theologians have sometimes overlooked evidence or the need for proof, as economic power and control can drive human actions beyond official doctrines.

The Rise of Scientific Dogma and Pseudoscience

While science prides itself on unbiased evidence and objectivity, it is susceptible to its own form of dogmatism. Pharmaceutical research highlights how scientific integrity can be compromised by economic interests. Studies unfavorable to pharmaceutical products often are still unpublished, biasing the available scientific literature (Turner et al., 2008). Similarly, the tobacco industry's manipulation of scientific research to obscure smoking's health risks shows how science can devolve into pseudoscience when profit motives prevail (Proctor, 2012).

Mainstream medicine provokes the most difficult conversations about science.

The Roots of Pharmacy

The word *pharmacy* has a fascinating etymology that winds through several languages, with varying degrees of meaning.

- **Greek origin**: It stems from the Ancient Greek word *pharmakeia*, which referred to the use of drugs, potions, or spells. This, in turn, comes from *pharmakon*, meaning drug, poison, or charm.
- The term carried dual connotations—both healing and harmful—reflecting the ancient belief that substances could cure or curse depending on intent and dosage.
- **Latin and French evolution**: It passed into Medieval Latin as *pharmacia*, and then into Old French as

31

farmacie, which referred to purgatives or medicinal substances.

- By the 14th century, English adopted *pharmacy* to mean medicinal treatment, and by the 17th century, it evolved to describe the practice of preparing and dispensing drugs.

Today, **pharmacy is associated with empirical scientific evidence aimed at improving health and alleviating discomfort.** The transformation of substances to accomplish this is complex and costly. Corporate marketing campaigns have promoted this perspective widely. Historically, advertising for pharmaceutical drugs on radio or television was either restricted by law or considered inconsistent with medical ethics.

Food and Drug Administration

The **prohibition of direct-to-consumer (DTC) pharmaceutical advertising on television was established decades ago** by regulatory practices in the United States, primarily through the Food and Drug Administration (FDA). Initially, strict FDA regulations dating back to 1969 mandated comprehensive disclosures regarding risks, side effects, and contraindications in advertisements. This complexity effectively limited drug advertising to professional associations, published in medical journals or through medical teaching channels and associated print media.

In 1985, the FDA began easing these restrictions by permitting drug advertisements to consumers under stringent conditions, still requiring extensive risk information. However, a significant shift occurred in 1997 when the FDA revised guidelines, allowing pharmaceutical companies to use television and radio for direct-to-consumer advertising by simplifying the risk disclosure requirements. Ads were then permitted to include a concise summary of risks along with directing consumers to toll-free numbers or websites for further information.

This regulatory change was driven by arguments that DTC advertising could empower consumers through awareness and education, fostering informed conversations with healthcare providers and potentially destigmatizing certain medical conditions. Conversely, critics expressed concerns over potential negative impacts, such as increased healthcare costs, inappropriate prescription drug use, and misleading or insufficiently balanced portrayals of medications.

Currently, the United States remains one of the few developed nations, alongside New Zealand, which allows extensive direct-to-consumer pharmaceutical advertising. Other countries continue to impose strict regulations or outright bans on such practices.

In summary, the historical trajectory from prohibition to the regulated permissiveness of direct to consumer (DTC) pharmaceutical advertising reflects ongoing debates about consumer empowerment, healthcare costs, medication usage, and public health implications. Meanwhile, it is extremely expensive for natural treatments that have little potential for profit incentives and are therefore unadvertised. The pharmaceutical industry lobby successfully motivated legislators to create other barriers, such as the prohibition of any claims to cure or treat diseases without FDA approvals, which is a high financial barrier.

Pharmaceutical drugs are marketed and sold with the primary aim to heal, and yet the research and distribution model that supports this industry is fundamentally a profit-generating enterprise. Companies dedicate billions of dollars toward discovering new drugs, but their motivation is not uniformly humanitarian. Instead, research is most often driven by market potential.

If a condition affects only a small population, few resources are allocated. In contrast, if a disease or symptom afflicts millions, research dollars flow in abundance. Without the expectations of a profitable outcome, little or no treatments emerge, regardless of genuine necessity and humanitarian needs.

This contradiction reveals the dual nature of pharmaceutical science: it has the capacity to both heal and harm. This duality is not merely theoretical. The process of bringing a drug to market often requires accepting some level of unintended consequence. *Side effects are minimized in advertising, and harm is rationalized as acceptable in service to the "greater good."* When the general population benefits, isolated cases of injury or death are considered statistical inevitabilities, not causes for halting distribution. This model allows physicians to prescribe medications with a guilt-free conscience—until undeniable evidence emerges showing harms exceeding intended benefits that cannot be ignored.

The Opioid Epidemic

No example illustrates this better than the opioid epidemic. The modern opioid crisis began in the late 1990s, when pharmaceutical companies such as Purdue Pharma aggressively marketed synthetic opioids like OxyContin. These drugs were promoted as safe, effective, and non-addictive when used for pain management. Doctors, relying on these claims, began prescribing opioids at unprecedented rates. Pain was declared the "fifth vital sign," and patients were increasingly rated on pain satisfaction scores. Medical professionals, under pressure to address pain comprehensively, leaned heavily on pharmaceutical solutions.

Marketing Strategies

Purdue's marketing strategies minimized addiction risks and emphasized patient satisfaction. This campaign was wildly successful: opioid prescriptions soared. By 2010, the widespread use of opioids had created a public health catastrophe. Millions became addicted to prescription medications. As prescriptions tightened in response, many individuals turned to cheaper, unregulated street opioids such as heroin and, more recently, fentanyl—a synthetic opioid 50 to 100 times more potent than morphine. Overdose deaths surged through misuse of these powerful drugs.

According to data from the Centers for Disease Control and Prevention (CDC), more than 564,000 people died from opioid overdoses between 1999 and 2020. The crisis has evolved into multiple waves: starting with prescription opioids, followed by heroin, and now dominated by synthetic opioids. As of 2023, fentanyl-related deaths continue to rise, contributing to an overall decline in U.S. life expectancy, especially within certain demographics.

The role of pharmaceutical companies, particularly Purdue Pharma, has come under intense scrutiny. In 2019, Purdue filed for bankruptcy and agreed to a multi-billion-dollar settlement with various state and local governments. The company's owners, the Sackler family, were eventually held accountable in public opinion if not criminal court and were ordered to contribute financially toward remediation efforts. **But the damage was already done.**

Healing And Harm—A Duality

At the center of the crisis lies a deeply flawed system that rewards marketing prowess over moral responsibility. The FDA, tasked with protecting public health, approved these drugs and allowed the marketing campaigns to proceed with insufficient scrutiny. Doctors, many of whom lacked adequate training in pain management or addiction risk, were incentivized to prescribe opioids liberally. Meanwhile, patients sought relief by engaging with a system that placed an emphasis on profit rather than patient wellbeing. This was a perfect formula for happiness through profitable enterprise and the distribution of great suffering—paradoxically patients were seeking freedom from pain.

Institutionalized Science for Profit

Science, in this case, did not fail because it lacked knowledge. It failed because the knowledge was corrupted by the pressures of commerce. Peer-reviewed journals published questionable data. Expert opinions were bought. Dissenters were discredited or silenced. The architecture of scientific credibility was used as a tool to bolster profit, not truth.

Unintended Consequences

Today, the duality of healing and harm persists. Pharmaceutical companies continue to innovate, but always through the lens of profitability. The development of life-saving drugs is now coupled with billion-dollar marketing campaigns. The cost of these drugs often places them out of reach for those who need them most.

Are chemical interventions a flawed belief system fundamentally driven by profit motivation?

If there is a lesson in the opioid epidemic, it is this: the integrity of science must be vigilantly protected from economic distortion. Regulatory agencies must act as true stewards of public health, not facilitators of corporate gain. Physicians must be trained not just in prescribing drugs, but in understanding their societal context and long-term consequences.

Most importantly, we must return to a moral framework in which healing is not just a commodity, but a sacred responsibility. Until that occurs, we will continue to see science used as a shield for systems that benefit from our suffering, rather than a beacon of light guiding us toward wellness. **The law of unintended consequences is hard at work.**

We must take control of our own health, and pharmaceutical profits will dimmish proportionately. Ultimately, everyone wins or loses depending upon how we act individually and collectively.

We must choose wisely—Forestry or Pharmacology.

For centuries, humans have derived medicine directly from plant sources. Ancient civilizations across the globe recognized forests as natural pharmacies, abundant with healing plants that alleviated illnesses and promoted health. These forests serve not only as reservoirs of life-sustaining nutrients and medicinal compounds but also as the lungs of the Earth—purifying the air, regulating climate, and maintaining ecological balance essential to our survival. Forests are complex, dynamic ecosystems teeming with biodiversity, playing critical roles in maintaining the stability of global environments.

In traditional medicine, plants have provided remedies for everything from minor discomfort to life-threatening conditions. Aspirin, one of the most widely used medicines, was originally derived from the bark of willow trees. The Pacific yew tree gave us Taxol, a powerful chemotherapy drug. More recently, Artemisia annua, a plant used in Chinese traditional medicine for centuries, yielded artemisinin, a compound vital in treating malaria. These examples underscore the vast pharmaceutical potential residing within natural ecosystems.

Yet, the intricate network of life within the forests, particularly the Amazon rainforest, is being dismantled at alarming rates. Every year, thousands of hectares are cleared for logging, agriculture, and livestock, causing irreversible damage to the biodiversity that holds potential cures to countless diseases. In recent decades, nearly 20% of the Amazon has been lost, and scientists warn that reaching a tipping point could turn vast portions of this lush habitat into dry savannah, drastically altering global climate patterns and limiting humanity's access to crucial medicinal resources.

The intersection of biotechnology, artificial intelligence (AI), and forest biodiversity presents an unprecedented opportunity. AI has the capacity to rapidly screen and analyze compounds from thousands of plant species, identifying potential new medicines far more efficiently than traditional methods. This computational power could unravel the complex biochemical properties of rainforest flora at an unprecedented scale, potentially discovering treatments for diseases currently deemed incurable. However, the acceleration of forest destruction may outpace our technological and scientific progress, leading to the extinction of species before they can be studied.

The destruction of forests is not merely an environmental issue; it is a profound loss of future medical innovation. Biodiversity is a reservoir of genetic diversity, essential for adaptability and resilience in the face of evolving diseases. Many pharmaceutical companies already acknowledge the importance of natural compounds in drug discovery. Yet, the conflict between short-term economic gains from logging and agriculture, and long-term pharmaceutical benefits remains a daunting challenge.

Current global efforts at conservation are insufficient. To ensure the sustainability of these invaluable resources, we must prioritize the preservation of forest ecosystems, balancing immediate economic interests against the long-term health benefits they provide. Investment in sustainable practices, stricter enforcement of conservation laws, and international cooperation are crucial for maintaining the integrity of forest biodiversity.

As we stand at this critical juncture, the question arises: Will we choose a path of short-sighted exploitation, risking the loss of irreplaceable resources, or will we commit to protecting and sustainably managing these vital ecosystems, securing both the ecological and medical well-being of future generations? The choice we make today—Forestry or Pharmacology—will shape the future of human health, ecological stability, and the planet itself.

Iatrogenesis—Death by Doctoring

Iatrogenesis refers to harm or illness caused by medical treatment or side effects cause by healthcare interventions.

This harm can occur due to errors in diagnosis, prescription of medications, surgical mistakes, hospital-acquired infections, or adverse effects of therapeutic procedures. Derived from Greek, "iatro" means physician or treatment, and "genesis" indicates creation, highlighting its roots as harm created inadvertently through medical care. Iatrogenic illness is a significant public health concern. According to various studies, medical errors and adverse events contribute substantially to mortality and morbidity. A landmark study published by Johns Hopkins University estimated that over 250,000 deaths annually in the United States are due to medical errors, making it the third leading cause of death, surpassed only by heart disease and cancer. Other research suggests that the actual number may exceed 400,000, which would position iatrogenesis as a leading cause of mortality.

In comparison, the Centers for Disease Control and Prevention (CDC) identify heart disease (approximately 700,000 deaths annually) and cancer (approximately 600,000 deaths annually) as the top two leading causes of death in the U.S.

This positions iatrogenesis prominently among critical health threats, surpassing deaths attributed to conditions such as respiratory diseases, stroke, Alzheimer's disease, diabetes, and influenza.

Recognizing the gravity of iatrogenic illness is crucial for promoting patient safety, improving healthcare quality, and guiding regulatory practices and healthcare policy to minimize preventable harm and enhance clinical outcomes.

Doctors Are People

Medicine has evolved into a group of believers that practice treatment protocols that are based on what they have been taught, rather than independent evaluation of evidence. Their *"evidence"* is rarely firsthand results, but theories are taught in medical schools—teachings with a foundation based on pharmacology—as thought to be based upon irrefutable evidence.

Doctors are people, so perfection is not expected—and many are open-minded to their patients' viewpoints. However, some doctors speak with great fervor and at times have expressed dismissive arrogance when confronted with contrarian beliefs. I worked at a hospital, and many people shared those experiences.

I have personally experienced gratifying encounters with the health care system, including life-changing surgical procedures. It is advisable to listen to the initial recommendations provided by health professionals but seek second opinions from other medical practitioners for a comprehensive understanding. Additionally, consider utilizing AI tools to enhance your knowledge and prepare pertinent questions for further clarification.

The Paradox of Scientific Progress and Human Happiness

Science has undeniably improved human conditions through technology and medicine, yet these advancements have not uniformly increased global happiness. The Easterlin Paradox reveals that increased wealth and technological advancement do not necessarily correlate with greater overall happiness (Easterlin, 1974). Societies experiencing economic growth often see static or declining measures of happiness, underscoring the limitation of science to address deeper emotional and existential human needs.

Facts for Faith as a Common Ground

Despite their perceived opposition, science and religion share a fundamental reliance on faith. The belief that evidence exists is how science develops faith. Religion openly acknowledges faith in unseen deities and metaphysical truths. Meanwhile, science implicitly depends on faith in consistent natural laws and rationality. Renowned physicist Paul Davies emphasizes that scientific endeavor is founded on the faith that nature is orderly and comprehensible, a belief not empirically provable but essential to scientific progress (Davies, 2007).

Furthermore, many scientific experiments result in evidence that cannot be independently replicated. This issue has become increasingly prevalent as financial incentives can influence human judgment. Universities provide fertile ground for researchers to explore new ideas, and sometimes these efforts yield correct results. However, pharmaceutical research is often driven by profit motives, which can compromise its integrity. As a result, medical research is not always perfect science, with unclear evidence and significant side effects that can be harmful, despite claims of being evidence-based.

Similarly, theologians are also human and have deliberately avoided public reading of scriptures that were not included in the canonized bibles used in religious services. Different religious groups hold varying beliefs, which can lead to the dismissal of each other's claims. The subjective nature of the human mind often leads individuals to prioritize self-interest over objective truth. Therefore, personal introspection is crucial rather than relying solely on unwavering faith.

People tend to seek comfort and belonging within their communities, often at the expense of independent thought and the pursuit of personal purpose. Science and religion share a fundamental self-evident tradition, each seeks to promote their institution as the definitive source of truth, and neither is willing admit their shortfalls.

I have decided to adopt a non-conformist approach, characterized by a strong reliance on intuition, mixed with a high degree of optimism and a healthy measure of skepticism. Navigating complex situations requires maintaining an upright posture while carefully advancing one step at a time.

Crisis of Confidence in Institutions

History repeatedly shows us that civilizations do not always collapse by external invasion—they collapse from within. The story of the Trojan Horse is more than a tale of military trickery; it is a metaphor for the ways we can willingly usher danger into our most sacred spaces. With fanfare, we roll the horse through the gates, pretending it is a gift, while knowing, somewhere deep within us, we knew that it concealed hidden threats.

So, it is with many institutions. Religion was embraced as a moral guide, yet too often harbored intolerance and abuse within its hallowed walls. Science promised objective truth, but economic incentives and political manipulation corrupted its impartiality.

We knew these dangers existed—we saw the arrogance of unchecked authority, the seduction of profit—but we opened the gates anyway. The result is a crisis of confidence.

A society that loses trust in its pillars feels betrayed not only by leaders but by the complicity of its citizens. We participated in our own disillusionment, tolerating the flaws for too long. Yet this crisis is not terminal, it is diagnostic. It reveals precisely where renewal must begin.

The Trojan Horse teaches us a paradox: what we invite in can destroy us, but it can also awaken us. When institutions falter, we are reminded that sovereignty cannot be outsourced. True transformation comes when individuals reclaim authorship of meaning, health, and truth. The crisis of confidence, painful as it is, is the threshold to self-responsibility.

A crisis of confidence ignites the flame as the situation gets too hot, and we must leap forward, not into cynicism, but into conscious design of a better future.

Seeking a Consensus

Agreement often feels comforting—but comfort rarely drives progress. Improvement arises through challenge, not compliance. When individuals seek consensus to validate their ideas, they risk diluting originality. While cooperation has value, universal agreement often leads to mediocrity, not creativity. Consensus tends to smooth out the edges of daring ideas, softening innovation into compromise.

History reminds us that greatness rarely emerges from group thinking. The most profound breakthroughs often originate from solitude, risk-taking, and courageous nonconformity. Originality demands a willingness to be misunderstood. Pioneers in every field—from science to art—first faced rejection before recognition. Their strength came not from consensus, but from clarity of vision.

True greatness arises when individuals embrace sovereignty over popularity, daring to explore paths that others fear. Independent thinking—not crowd approval—is the fertile ground where exceptional ideas grow. Creative energy must be protected during its incubation by ignoring former beliefs.

Consensus has its place in teamwork and policy making but should not restrain innovation. Original thought is fragile in its early stages and requires protection from the pressures of conformity. Committees may organize and refine, but they do not originate genius.

In conclusion, greatness is not forged through collective agreement but through personal conviction. Consensus may guide shared action, but it rarely ignites transformation. Let originality stand apart—allow it time and space to evolve. Only then can it rise beyond mediocrity and shape a future worthy of its potential.

Personal Story: Doctrine of Self-Reliance

As the first born, son and namesake of my father, I was initiated into a legacy steeped in independence, ingenuity, and resolute self-reliance. From an early age, my father—a true "jack of all trades" embodied the principle that adaptability and creativity are the keys to transcending any challenge. He instilled in me the belief that a lazy man plays tricks on himself, where his limitations are only beliefs held within the confines of his mind. This philosophy ignited a determination within me that became deeply ingrained in my character.

One vivid childhood memory still stands as a defining moment. When I proudly proclaimed to my elementary school teacher, Mrs. Brennen, "I can do anything," her approving smile affirmed that my ideals were not only achievable but also celebrated. Later on, I gathered every dictionary in our home, fervently **searching for the words "cannot" and "can't," only to strike them through with deliberate strokes of my pen**. In my youth, this act represented an unyielding commitment to possibility and ambition.

First Born Alpha Male Lion

An unwavering self-confidence has remained a cornerstone of my identity— and sometimes this becomes a fault. Born under the astrological sign of Leo, the lion, I embody its spirit—bold, fearless, and unapologetically authentic. As my father once said, "I am the man that I am", and nothing could be truer. He didn't rely upon the "likes" or the approval of others, and he always honored his obligations to family, friends and his employers. **Agreements were made with a handshake, and that became a commitment in lieu of a written contract.**

44

Now, I am polishing my skills, ambitions, and designs for humanity such that individuals become as bright as stars, as they in turn enlighten their communities and eventually change the world through spirit science.

Advice from Cats

The analogy "Advice from Cats" deeply resonates with my family doctrine. Cats, by nature, exemplify autonomy and a large measure of self-confidence. They remain undisturbed by external opinions, navigate through life's unpredictability with graceful adaptability, and instinctively know when to assert themselves or when to patiently observe. Like a cat, I have learned to trust my instincts, remain authentic in my interactions, and *appreciate solitude* as a space for creative reflection and personal growth.

Ralph Waldo Emerson's seminal essay "Self-Reliance," encountered during my high school years, profoundly reinforced these familial lessons. Emerson's wisdom resonated deeply: responsible action emerges not from the conformity and consensus of the majority, but from independent contemplation and intuitive wisdom. True self-reliance, he wrote, means embracing one's own judgment, and daring to carve a unique path through life's complex terrain, despite societal pressures to conform. Our greatest achievement is being authentic with ourselves and choosing a path that keeps us aligned with self-directed principles, morals, and a code of conduct that respects everyone's rights to the same freedoms and independence.

This doctrine has consistently informed me through various challenges. My background spans suspended academic pursuits, entrepreneurial initiatives, and inquiry across multiple disciplines—including science, mathematics, and the creative arts—which has strengthened my conviction that versatility, adaptability, and independent thinking are critical for overcoming adversity. Creativity often stands in stark contrast to conformity. While mistakes have been unavoidable, each misstep has provided valuable insight, enabling course correction and renewed motivation.

Rejecting the idea of being pigeonholed into a singular skill set, I adopted my father's pragmatic yet imaginative approach to problem-solving. This meant **courageously venturing into varied disciplines, being a jack-of-all-trades, always willing to redefine and reinvent my understanding**. The conviction that solutions are often found in unexpected intersections between different fields has led me to pursue broad knowledge and versatile capabilities, proving that authentic creativity thrives beyond narrow boundaries.

Thus, the essence of our family doctrine is rooted firmly in self-reliance, creative independence, and limitless thinking. It champions personal authenticity and the courage to diverge from mainstream opinions. It celebrates versatility over specialization, creativity over conformity, and intuition over convention.

Ultimately, like the quiet confidence of a cat, it reminds us to trust our instincts, remain agile and curious, and always believe unwaveringly in our capacity to overcome limitations—**to live boldly, independently, and without ever uttering "I can't."**

Reconciliation Through Spirit Science

My life's work has been engaged to reconcile my parents' religion with my professor's science teachings. At multiple stages in life my learning has waved to either one or the other side of these differing points of view. The merger of those seeming oppositions is spirit science that tells us both how and why we should practice spirit science, because it is a new kind of knowledge. Whatever our choices have been before coming to discover this, we aren't bound to a doctrine that punishes us for disbelief or subjected to peer reviews that reject our intuition.

We must come to understand that every belief we choose shapes a unique and personal subconscious experience. Following the narratives of others—whether ancient bible stories that explore the past or modern research studies that weave evidence into a storyline—cannot guarantee alignment with the distinctive circumstances of individual lives. Neither faith nor facts alone can universally guide everyone toward inner happiness.

Our likes, fears, desires, and motives are profoundly influenced by the relationships we form, beginning in childhood and evolving throughout adulthood. These experiences define who we are and reveal the origins of love in our lives. Love, as the ultimate creative force, unites two individuals in harmony, much like a gravitational field drawing spirits together to create a new life.

True happiness, as well as health and well-being, must originate from within each of us. Fear, born of countless factors, touches each of us differently, but it consistently acts as a destructive force. The only undeniable truth lies in the choices we make—between creating and destroying. Our decisions and our actions have consequences, and this principle is irrefutable. Heal thyself is my chosen belief. Happiness, health and wealth are interconnected, and we can experience them both individually and in unity with the broader society.

Neither science nor religion has proven to be a panacea for the human condition. Religion has inspired extraordinary compassion and insight, yet also intolerance and war. Religion seeks answers to existential questions, yet those answers differ wildly and irreconcilably across cultures. This can also be seen among people that decry the same fundamental belief yet find a subtle point of view that contradicts a fellow parishioner, and yet another branch of church pews is made—separated from the previous branch.

Science has vastly expanded our grasp of the universe and improved life's conveniences, yet it has not solved the

47

riddle of happiness or erased humanity's capacity for folly; Science unveils profound truths, yet each discovery opens new questions. The misuse of science can sow doubt and distrust. **The world today is not universally happier or more truthful for having both churches and laboratories**. It remains a complex embroidery—weaving belief and skepticism, enlightenment and ignorance, hope and anxiety. This does not mean the efforts of religion and science have been in vain; on the contrary, each has illuminated important facets of human existence. But it does mean that **no single system has all the answers**.

"Man cannot live by bread alone – he cannot live by science alone, either." Nor, it appears, can he live by faith alone in our pluralistic world."— C.S. Lewis

---

In the end, the limitations of science and religion may counsel a measure of humility. Rather than pinning humanity's salvation on one or the other, we might recognize that both have something to contribute, and both have something to learn. Religion can temper science with ethics and meaning; science can temper religion with critical inquiry and shared empirical standards. Both, at their best, encourage awe and wonder at truths greater than us. A truly **universally happier and more truthful world** might emerge not from choosing between science and religion, but from an honest dialogue that acknowledges the strengths and shortcomings of each. Until then, the quest for absolute truth and lasting happiness goes on – a journey as old as our species, charted by the light of reason and the wisdom of faith in tandem, even as final certainty lies perpetually beyond the horizon.

The Intangibility of Absolute Truth

Neither science nor religion has provided absolute truths universally accepted by humanity. Religious doctrines diverge significantly, each asserting its version of absolute truth, resulting in a fragmented global religious landscape. In science, truths are provisional, continually revised or overturned as new evidence emerges. Philosopher Thomas Kuhn highlighted science's shifting paradigms, illustrating that scientific truths are not permanent but evolve through revolutionary shifts in understanding (Kuhn, 1962).

Conclusion

We must refrain from seeking external validation and listening to institutional guidelines in our pursuit of truth, particularly when aiming to discern an absolute and irrefutable truth. While practical advice is best sought from experts, our life purpose necessitates inward reflection and contemplation; this is the path to finding happiness. Engaging our own experiential perspectives, along with cultivating inner peace, allows us to develop sufficient maturity to seek and articulate our own version of truth.

It is crucial to undertake this journey without feeling compelled to convince others of our beliefs. Our childhood experiences have often indoctrinated us with the beliefs of our parents, relatives, neighbors, friends, and the broader community in which we were raised. We must learn to write each new chapter of our lives, and this process becomes more manageable once we understand the foundations of human thought. **Actions we take set the stage, and we design the direction of life's purpose with imagination and vigor. Only then can we become fully engaged and unstoppable.**

Buckle up, you are on a journey where reflection about beliefs and personal challenges will come soon enough. But keep an open mind in knowing that nothing worthwhile comes from standing still, except rainfall and wet conditions where flowers or weeds can grow. Flowers grow where we have carefully put effort into tending them. Weeds take on the life of their own choosing.

Continuous comparison with others does not facilitate personal advancement; therefore, it is important to assert individual autonomy. This approach is not intended as a rejection of broader society, but rather as a method to enable individuals to make their fullest contributions without unnecessary hindrances. Relying on the assumption that others possess superior ideas or will compensate for our shortcomings is limiting.

Each person bears responsibility for achieving the highest standard their abilities allow, independent of external validation or subordination. Embracing personal sovereignty enables one to live and reflect with the assurance that their efforts were maximized.

It is not necessary to rely on constant competition with others as a means of advancement; instead, individuals can focus on their own development. This approach does not require separation from society but aims to create opportunities for individual contributions without unnecessary obstacles.

Personal accountability involves making the most of one's abilities without relying on others to compensate or offer approval, and without subordinating to external authority. Moral concepts such as fairness and treating others as we wish to be treated are learned early in life and can guide interactions within a community. These principles allow for self-improvement that does not come at the expense of others.

People want to talk about what they believe, so let them. It will be useless debate trying to elevate your independence, whilst trying to convince others to follow your beliefs in contradictions with theirs. Time well spent is by developing proof that our ideas truly work to our advantage, by example, with or without approvals or a consensus. We should live and die with the knowledge that we have done our best. Becoming a sovereign individual is a way to find your pathway to personal transformation, and ultimately becoming supernatural is a lifestyle, not playing the role of a Hollywood character.

Our pathway to personal transformation will be developed from basics and steadily progress into greater proof using philosophical and scientific rationale. Supernatural power is attainable, but determination and effort are required for personal metamorphosis.

Chapter 2: The Pathway to Personal Transformation

Introduction—Preparing Your Internal Soil

Awareness becomes the lens through which change becomes not just visible, but actionable. In this stage, we are preparing the internal soil. The mind must be focused and emotionally stabilized and these are prerequisites, just as sunshine and water in soil germinates plants. Wakefulness is the seed from which all mental and spiritual growth emerges.

Personal Story: The Belief That I Can Do Anything

I can recall the very moment that my self-confidence was planted. As a 5th grader, my teacher, Mrs. Brennan, asked if I could help organize a mess of books and supplies left scattered by classmates. I smiled and responded without hesitation, *"I can do anything."*

"Whether you think you can, or you think you can't, you're right." — Henry Ford

---

First Seeds of Confidence

She handed me a more difficult task—and I accepted it with the same attitude, even though a quiet voice inside me questioned whether I could alphabetize the books correctly. I gave it my full attention, and my success ignited something deeper: belief in myself eliminated doubts. Later, when I proudly declared to my mother that "can't" was no longer in my vocabulary, she promptly asked me to clean the bathroom.

The Story of "C.A.P."

After completing that chore, *I announced that the bathroom was "C.A.P." – Clean As Possible*. That moment became our family code. "CAP" wasn't just about cleaning—it became a symbol of my determination and self-assigned accountability. From then on, when something was done to the best of our ability, it was declared to be C.A.P.

These were early childhood transformations into self-responsibility that illustrate the principle of mindfulness in action—when we begin to see ourselves not as victims of circumstance but as architects of possibility. Transformation begins with a story we tell ourselves—and believe.

Awareness Precedes Transformation

Some readers could find themselves taking their first steps to become aware of their unfocused structure of thought, and that might feel uncomfortable. Awareness is necessary before we start planting seeds and moving onto higher ground. The elevation rises as you find breadcrumbs at the beginning of our climb, then stop, nurture food for thought, and finally propelling us up a metaphorical stairway to heaven on earth.

We eventually understand the mind, body, spirit and soul can be subdivided into pieces, like a pile of bricks awaiting mortar to build the wall. Then we tune each part and put them back together to reveal ourselves as supernatural beings. That is how metaphysical principles come together and get applied into spirit science. Let's look at how basic transformation and growth begins.

Transformation begins with a single spark of awareness, the moment when we recognize that change is not only possible, but essential. Personal transformation does not happen by accident. It requires conscious engagement,

54

emotional fuel, consistent action, and inner accountability. In this chapter, we will examine a six-stage framework for personal growth that combines emotional energy, structured thinking, and practical steps to guide the reader from self-awareness to sustained mastery.

The alignment of our intention with behavior causes transformation. It is the maturation of thought into sustained, repeatable patterns of success. True change begins internally, but becomes visible externally through our actions, networking our relationships, improving physical health, and controlling emotional states.

To become transformed is to shift from routine habitual living to intentional becoming—where continuous improvements are the norm and happiness becomes habitual. Transformation is also required when, at first, failure has been met, and we must retreat to collect our thoughts and go forward again and again.

As we begin forming new habits, the process often reveals hidden internal conflicts. When our stated values clash with our behaviors, the tension we experience is called *cognitive dissonance*, a powerful psychological force that can either stall us in place or propel us toward meaningful change. If we are willing to confront this dissonance with honesty and structure, we unlock a deeper level of transformation.

The following personal account illustrates how I confronted my own inner conflict—between a long-standing habit and a deep desire for health. It was not willpower alone that carried me forward, but the creation of a narrative and a method of self-accountability that reframed my identity. What began as a health crisis became a turning point—an awakening to the power of intentional discipline and emotional clarity.

Personal Story: Cognitive Smoke—The Discipline of Day Counting

In December 1989, after fifteen years of smoking, I confronted an unavoidable truth: I was killing myself, and I knew it. A pack of cigarettes contained **20 cigarettes** and most importantly there were only 24 hours in a day. If memory serves me accurately, there were 10 packs in a carton, but I rarely bought single packages, except in case of an emergency where my Kool brand was unavailable. Sometimes, I try to get more out of a single day, but 1 ½ up to two (2) packages were consumed daily on average. The above illustration shows a person ready to break the chain-smoking habit, contemplating metamorphosis of the butterfly.

I SMOKED ONE CIGARETTE EVERY HALF-HOUR—NON STOP—EXCEPT SLEEPING AND EATING WERE ALSO NECESSITIES.

My periodontist had diagnosed me with periodontal disease and scheduled surgery for February of the coming year. That news ignited a battle within me—a classic case of cognitive dissonance. On the one hand, I valued health and on the other, I was clinging to a self-destructive habit. The internal tension was unbearable. I lit my first cigarette every morning over the ashes of my last, tethered to a ritual that gave me nothing but the illusion of control. For a long time, I told myself, "I can quit at any time."

I had tried many times before and failed. But this time, I needed a story strong enough to reshape my identity.

56

So, I MADE A DECISION: I WOULD NOT SMOKE A SINGLE CIGARETTE DURING THE ENTIRE DECADE OF THE 1990S. Everyone must write their story. That long horizon gave the resolution more weight and meaning, while dangling the notion that it wasn't forever. On New Year's Eve 1989, I smoked my final cigarette.

At midnight, I began **_Day One of abstinence_** and committed to counting each day. If I relapsed, I would reset the count back to zero. To break my mental associations, I discarded every hidden pack—from the trunk of the car to the back of kitchen drawers. No more escape hatches. That last carton of cigarettes was gone!

The Discipline of Counting Upward

By the eleventh day, the withdrawal symptoms had escalated to a severe psychological challenge. That night, I experienced intense craving and nervous tremors, contemplating a visit to a gas station for a pack of KOOLs. I was aware of the tobacco industry's historical claims that cigarettes were harmless and did not cause cancer. Despite acknowledging that some individuals have lived long lives while smoking, knowing also that many more have died. My cognitive dissonance led to internal conflicts between seeking pleasure and exercising self-control for better health. What was the actual truth? Which belief aligned more closely with achieving success?

But I held my ground, clenching beneath the sheets in mental agony—as sleep finally arrived and the birds had begun singing. When I finally woke up, it was past noon on Thursday afternoon. Panic set in: I had missed work without calling in. As a professional, a Database Administrator, this was unthinkable.

My mind raced, trying to invent a plausible excuse. Instead, I chose honesty. I called Desmond Maddens, my boss, and told him the truth—that I was battling to quit smoking. To my amazement, Desi responded with kindness and support. He said he was proud of me. That moment of grace reinforced my commitment.

Reflecting back, I see how smoking had conditioned me. We smoked at our desks, lit up in meetings, shared cigarettes like social currency. Quitting was not just breaking a habit but dismantling an identity. As the smoke finally cleared, my identity was reborn, I had kept my word to myself, proving that self-discipline could be applied to everything. I knew how to count sit-ups and push-ups from years prior working my body into physical fitness.

Mediocrity stems from the avoidance or acknowledgment of personal shortcomings. Although bad habits may persist, their consequences gradually surface, often unnoticed until it is too late to mitigate them. These consequences become evident in the fullness of time. Self-improvement necessitates courage and commitment.

Successful individuals habitually monitor their progress. Without tracking our advancements, we lose the opportunity for measurable improvements. While each day arrives without effort, tomorrow can be better than yesterday if we strive toward meaningful changes.

Interestingly, that same year, without knowing it was Lent, I began my first fast. I went eleven days without a regular meal, ate one banana, then continued for four more days. I counted those days too, building discipline and a new sense of self. By the month of July, the cigarette cravings were gone. I had avoided smoky bars and friends who still smoked. I had rewritten the story of who I was—a man who chooses health over habit, even in the face of inner conflict.

The Spark of Conscious Change

Stage 1: Awareness

Mindfulness is the first key to transformation. It creates the mental clarity to observe our habits, thoughts, and emotions without judgment. Only by seeing clearly can we begin to choose deliberately. However, seeing is visionary, but emotional excitement is like kindling put underneath the larger logs, where a burning desire can turn into a bonfire of deliberate and sustainable actions.

- Mindfulness begins to establish what we want to change.
- Emotions arise to help us envision new outcomes.
- Human energy is created and directed by emotional clarity.
- A burning desire is a form of free energy that fuels our imagination.

Awareness becomes the lens through which change becomes not just visible, but actionable. In this stage, we are thinking and preparing to taking action. Wakefulness is the seed from which all growth emerges.

We begin to observe our behaviors and choices as if viewed from outside ourselves. This detachment enables honest evaluation. The greatest changes in life begin with noticing something we can no longer ignore and detaching our emotions.

The Alchemy of Vision

Stage 2: Imagination and Energy

Imagination is the creative force of the mind. It gives shape and direction to emotional energy, transforming vision into intention. When aligned with emotional energy, it becomes a forge where transformation is shaped.

- Imagination is a fireplace where solutions are forged.
- Inventors, artists, and pioneers begin with a spark of inspiration.
- Writing ideas on paper is the ignition of transformation.
- Nothing meaningful is created without energy.

Creative energy, aligned with vision, becomes a forward-moving force. Dreams build a workshop in the mind. The mind responds to emotional desire by creating images, concepts, and blueprints of new realities. Visualization is a skill that anyone can develop, and it empowers us to mentally rehearse outcomes before we begin working. When a vision is vivid enough, and reinforced regularly, the subconscious begins to aim its emotional energy to align with that vision.

The Machinery of Transformation

Stage 3: Habit Formation

Transformation takes root in repetition. Habits are the architecture of our lives, either lifting us up or holding us down.

- It takes approximately 30 days to form a new habit.
- Poor habits form effortlessly; good habits require sustained effort.
- You must hold yourself accountable for both good and bad habits.
- Believing that change will occur without action is self-deception.

Changing a habit changes your life. Habits act like software algorithms running silently in the background of consciousness. If we program these algorithms intentionally, they will work for us instead of against us. We must replace disempowering behaviors with empowering routines—step by step, day by day, and through consistent reinforcement.

Turning Thought into Form

Stage 4: Action and Reinforcement

Thought without action is fantasy. Action is how we materialize the internal vision into external outcomes. Without deliberate action, old habits are retained. Written tasks leading to action moves us forward.

- Task completion feels good and builds momentum.
- Emotions must grow stronger to sustain long-term change.
- Task lists provide structure and reinforcement.
- An accountability ledger turns intention into measurable outcomes.

Small, consistent actions become habits; habits shape destiny. Self-talk programs the subconscious mind to make us think differently, and even the smallest works carry-forward into increasing momentum.

Building an Internal System

Stage 5: Accountability and Structure

Transformation must be supported by personal structure. Like financial ledgers track money, emotional and behavioral ledgers track self-mastery. You must establish a record keeping system, a diary where daily journaling will help to leave a trail of evidence. This was a lesson I learned as an insurance sales associate, where keeping score demonstrates a commitment to progress. Losing means to never keep score, whereas winners keep score by recording all of their efforts.

- Record tasks and habits in a personal journal.
- Use written notes or ledgers to track outcomes.
- Success begins with clarity, grows with passion, and is fulfilled through action.
- Daily rituals reinforce your personal values.

Structure is the invisible scaffolding that holds transformation in place. Formation of plans are discipline's ally. Without calendars, journals and systems, even great effort is soon lost to chaos. Just as engineers draft blueprints, we must create systems to track our effort and adjust our strategies. Routines are scaffolding that elevates the vision into reality.

Becoming Who You Want to Be

Stage 6: Sustained Growth

True transformation is not a one-time event but a lifelong pursuit. The goal is not perfection, but slow, deliberate routines for advancement.

- Momentum builds strength, but purpose gives meaning.
- Tracking progress helps sustain forward motion.
- Accountability to others strengthens accountability to self.
- Mastery is the ability to control emotions and direct actions intentionally.

Growth becomes sustainable when it is rooted in conscious choice, personal alignment, and emotional maturity. Sustained growth emerges when change becomes our lifestyle. This is the transformation of identity. We become someone who no longer needs reminders or external discipline—our inner compass leads us forward with calm confidence. This is not about motivation but integration of our dreams to weave the fabric of our future, where the self becomes the primary, not the reactor.

Personal Story: Becoming a Thousandaire

This book is the culmination of a lifelong quest to understand the deeper nature of personal success, thought, and human potential.

From an early age, I was fueled by a relentless curiosity. I wasn't satisfied with traditional explanations or the limitations society placed on people. I became a bookworm, reading hundreds of books—far beyond those assigned in school—seeking answers wherever I could find them.

After a brief stint working for Equitable Life Assurance Society, it became clear that selling life insurance wasn't the right fit. The job was demanding, the income unpredictable, and entirely commission-based. Despite my ambition and enthusiasm, I struggled financially and eventually fell deeply into credit card debt. Eventually, I was summoned to the manager's office and was told to clear my desk of any personal belongings—I was fired, after a 24-month tryout. And I had previously worked 2 years with Investors Diversified Services, selling Mutual Funds and Insurance. I didn't have the emotional maturity for commissioned-only sales.

I had to give up my apartment and move back into my parents' home. I carried little more than personal belongings, a few furnishings, and a small library of books. My briefcase still had a copy of Napoleon Hill's "*Think And Grow Rich*", Morton Shulman's well-worn book, "*Anyone Can Still Become a Millionaire—Investing in Stocks*", and some loose change in my pockets.

That's when my mother said something I'll never forget, "Why not try to become a Thousandaire first?"

Her advice was practical—and I was humbled. She also offered to help with college tuition so I could go back and finish my degree. I spent the following months immersed in books at the public library. Ironically, I read more during that time—while unemployed—than I ever had before. Swallowing my pride, I realized going back to college was not a step backward—it was a strategic restart.

The lofty goal of becoming a millionaire had not been abandoned, it was simply deferred. In that moment, the idea of becoming a **thousandaire** became the first milestone in my new journey of transformation.

I was already reading *John Naisbitt's book, Megatrends* in which he explored the major societal shifts shaping the future. Published in 1982, the book identified key transformations, including the transition from an industrial society to an information-driven future. I peered into that book like a crystal ball, as it forecasted my future. ***Jobs that included analytical thinking would become a strength***, unlike sales that depended on attributes that were my weaknesses.

A former sales manager remarked that I was ***"slow and methodical"***, which was not complimentary. Yet I reflected upon his opinion, developing an awareness of how my natural ability could help me achieve success.

I had to ***reinvent myself***, and this sparked my imagination, becoming the key motivation that redefined my career path. I changed my college major to computer science, where precise thinking is essential for crafting software algorithms. Failure, adversity and a major shift in attitude led to many life-changing transformations. Artificial intelligence is causing another societal shift, and many people will be forced to reinvent themselves.

Conclusion—The Empowered Self

The pathway to personal transformation is both structured and organic. It begins with awareness and ends with mastery, but each step along the way demands attention, intention, and action. By applying this mental model, you do not merely improve your life—you recreate yourself. You evolve into a person of clear vision, focused energy, strong habits, purposeful action, and unwavering accountability.

This is not only the path to personal success, it's the first step on the road to becoming supernatural. Each reader must find models that resonate with their personal needs or mental frameworks.

We will integrate mental models in the broader framework of the architecture of consciousness. Each stage is a bridge towards higher cognitive function, spiritual awareness, and alignment with universal principles.

Chapter 3: Foundations for the Architecture of Consciousness

Introduction—Thinking Deeply

Have you ever stopped to wonder how your thoughts shape your reality?

This book explores the fascinating connections between consciousness, your mind, your brain, and the world around you. It will guide you on a journey where science, religion, philosophy, and everyday life are combined to reveal that your thoughts have incredible power. Your thoughts create your experiences. Everything you see—from your smartphone to buildings—started as someone's idea—just a single thought.

Your own thoughts can shape your friendships, academic or employment success, and **most importantly your health**. To manifest, means that spiritual power is involved. Humans have progressed to become spiritual beings, and we have developed physical structures within our brains that give us a unique ability for direct linkages between the mental realm into the physical realm.

We will explore vibrational frequencies, harmonic ratios, and consciousness engineering. This foundational structure will continue to serve as a practical roadmap for the reader's inner and outer evolution. What now becomes possible is **to take full control of our thoughts, and then we become architects of mind over matter.**

Personal Story: Johnny-Come-Lately — A Daydreamer's Redemption

Our thoughts—both structured and unstructured—shape how we interpret and engage with the world. Yet not all thinking follows rigid timelines or prescribed paths.

As a junior high school student, I was labeled "Johnny-come-lately" by one teacher who noticed I was always a bit behind on assignments. I was a daydreamer, someone who preferred to sit with ideas, turning them over in my mind until they revealed something deeper.

Though it may have looked like procrastination, I eventually came to see it differently. Those wandering thoughts weren't a weakness—they were the prelude to innovation. I wasn't mentally slow. I was thorough. I was deliberate. And I was deeply curious.

The Slow Mind That Sees Deeply

In hindsight, that daydreaming was part of how I formed new ways of thinking, unconstrained by deadlines or the need for rapid validation. Ideas needed time to mature, to ferment quietly beneath the surface before rising to the top with clarity and depth. I was never one to chase rapid answers—I was the one who stayed with each question longer.

That nickname, meant as a slight, evolved into a source of personal pride. My slower deliberate pace became my power. I learned to honor my own rhythm. And as the years unfolded, I realized that many of the innovations I would later develop began not with urgency, but with the steadiness of quiet contemplation.

The architecture of consciousness begins here—with the realization that even our perceived flaws can become strengths when placed in the right context. The key lies in reframing our self-perception to empower growth, not inhibiting it, or allowing others to trample upon our dreams.

The Soul Initiative

At the precise moment when a single sperm penetrates the ovum, a biological miracle begins. What science observes as a calcium wave and genetic fusion, ancient wisdom views as something even more profound—the spark of being—a soul arrives in the physical domain. Two strands of DNA entwine, but something more than chemistry ignites the unfolding of life.

Might this be the moment the soul arrives—not as a chemical, but as a traveler, a witness, a rider mounting the horse of form? This metaphor speaks to something long-intuited across cultures: that human life begins not merely with cellular multiplication, but with the infusion of purpose, awareness—and later we will discover, a yet-unnamed energy.

DNA is often thought of as the blueprint of life, a molecular instruction set passed from parent to child. But this dual helix—half from the mother, half from the father—does not explain the full emergence of personhood. Consciousness, that inner witness, cannot be reduced to genes. Nor can the soul, whose origin lies outside material analysis. The threefold nature of life, as I propose, arises from this trinity: the body formed by DNA, the mind shaped by experience and pattern, and the soul as the initiating force. This model reflects my Factor-9 philosophy—a balance of three elements, harmonizing to create not just life, but meaning.

Mindfulness works at its own pace, as appropriate for the circumstances being observed or contemplated. Urgent problems must be resolved, however, the childhood

67

story/fable about the rabbit and the turtle will serve us well in many ways. To illustrate the power of mindfulness and intention in shaping reality, we need food for thought: the slow steady pace of the turtle brings about clarity. And the following fable illustrates the power of the mind in a completely different way.

Fictional Story: The Weaver of Destiny

In an ancient kingdom, there was *a woman known as the Weaver of Destiny.* She was neither queen nor noble, yet the people whispered that her tapestries held mystical power. It was said that whatever she wove into fabric would manifest into reality.

One day, a skeptical scholar visited the Weaver, demanding proof of her ability. She handed him a blank piece of cloth and said, "What you see before you is nothing, yet within it lies infinite potential. What you choose to weave will decide what becomes."

The scholar hesitated, then carefully wove an image of a thriving village with golden fields and peaceful streets. Weeks later, when he returned home, he found that his struggling town had begun to prosper—new crops flourished, and the community thrived as if an invisible hand had guided it.

Realizing the truth behind her words, the scholar asked, "How did this happen?"

The Weaver replied, **"Reality does not merely happen to us. It is woven by our thoughts, our focus, and our intent. The world reflects what the mind consistently envisions."**

Like the Weaver, we craft our destiny through the architecture of consciousness. What we choose to focus on, **whether consciously or subconsciously**, influences the outcomes we experience.

What is Thought, Really?

Thought is the fabric of our reality, more than just something that occurs inside your brain, it's a powerful tool you can use to create your future. Everything you see around you, from your phone to buildings, started as someone's idea. Your thoughts, too, can shape the reality you experience. All things become possible with a plan based on ideas that often originate in our dreams. We start by programming our minds to design solutions, drawing from existing knowledge or creating breakthroughs others never imagined possible.

Whether working independently or with others, our imaginations support the foundation of all human achievements. **The architecture of our thoughts give direction to our dreams and builds the courage to realize them.** While we are dreaming our sub-conscious mind gets reconnected to the entirety of universal consciousness, where unlimited creative potential exists, and we a joined by every other individual that is tuning their thoughts on the same channel that we are tuned. Universal consciousness hosts a zoom meeting, where all are welcomed to listen or speak.

Personal Story: Finding My Own Path

During my youth, I aspired to become a medical doctor. However, as I matured, I came to understand that the field of medicine did not align with my first perceptions—born in the naivety of youth. Rather than focusing exclusively on genuinely healing individuals, the medical profession primarily emphasizes the diagnosis of conditions and the prescription of medications.

It soon became clear that prescription drug therapies were mainstream medicine's foundational belief, and healing was only in principle, never a promise in fact. Treatments could never become the promise of healing. I was unwilling to follow that reality, and being powerless to change university, I quit to become a college drop-out at the start of my senior year at WSU.

I had developed an insight, believing that true healing couldn't possibly lead to side effects and would require a holistic approach, addressing the well-being of the entire person—mind, body, and spirit. As a result, I found myself in search of an alternative career path that resonated more closely with my values. And I wanted a high paying career to earn a good living.

Independent thought forms the core structure of an awakened mind, allowing individuals to transcend external conformity and realize their highest creative potential.

Self-Reliance and Non-Conformity

True awakening demands more than intellectual understanding—it requires personal sovereignty. The spirit science framework rests upon self-reliance and conscious non-conformity. Drawing from my high school literature course: reading **Ralph Waldo Emerson's concept of Self-Reliance**, I recognized that societal conformity often obscures intuition and diminishes creative potential.

To become supernatural is to reclaim independent thought, to trust one's internal guidance above external validations, and to courageously shape a life resonant with personal truth rather than institutional expectations.

Throughout my twenties, I traversed different paths whilst designing and reconsidering my life purpose many times, using intuitions and thoughtful planning to guide me toward worthwhile goals. Life-changing lessons were learned and ultimately, my dreams and ambitions were met with happiness and success.

A Continuous Journey

Starting any journey requires a roadmap that indicates our current location and the path to our destination. Ambitious journeys necessitate careful planning and may require new tools for understanding the various languages encountered along the way, and especially at the end of the journey. Changing oneself fundamentally begins with an uphill course, but waypoints along the route provide methods to prepare for each subsequent step.

Each step and every milestone in this journey is backed by a mathematical, psychological, neuroscience or spiritual rationale, and while we attempt to go straightforward, it asks for engagement and effort to maximize the benefits promised and hopefully you are seeking. The goal is to develop personal mastery and enhance supernatural abilities using key theories and then practical methods and tactics for success. Not everyone will attain supernatural power—not because they can't—on the contrary, because they are afraid to be seen by others as unique or different.

Let's begin slowly from where you are, and gradually, we explore as the deeper meaning and understanding of important underlying principles, and then address how supernatural powers are developed from within. Soon enough, we'll **develop practical tactics and actions to practice spirit science** in a way that will be easy. Practice begins after we learn, "why it works", and then rules of the game will help us to fully develop our inner strengths, while standing on a solid foundation—you can develop greater confidence based in facts or faiths—to realize your greatest strengths and purpose.

The Sacred Science of Number

This guide develops and explores spirit science through ancient history, modern culture and scientific beliefs. The concept of "spirit science" doesn't have a single, definitive

71

author. It often refers to the blending of scientific principles with spiritual ideas, and various thinkers have contributed to this idea. Understanding mind-body-soul interface does not require advanced math or science knowledge or degrees. There are no exams or memorization requirements; you can learn at your own pace. However, math does underpin nature and physical reality.

Ancient cultures discovered numbers through reflection, seeing them as vibrational essences with cosmological power. In harmonic cosmology, we recognize that **numbers represent qualities, not just quantities**. The cosmos is a symphony of numerical songs, with light and sound vibrating along the electromagnetic spectrum, reaching our eyes and ears, and then our brains interpret these **qualia** as information. Numbers reveal the interconnected patterns and rhythms of the universe, from planetary orbits to subatomic particles. Mathematics serves as the unifying score for these phenomena, showcasing harmony and order in nature. The electromagnetic spectrum reveals all the musical octaves at play somewhere in the cosmos—each octave has specific qualities and provides us with information.

We must decipher the meaning of each electromagnetic signal—is that a star radiating light, a planet reflecting sunlight or a distant galaxy? Visible light occurs within the electromagnetic spectrum.

Numeracy refers to the ability to understand, interpret, and work with numbers in everyday life. It's more than just basic math skills that we use numbers—not simply for counting things—it involves reasoning with qualitative information, not solving problems, or making decisions based on numerical data. Being numerate does also enable an individual to manage tasks such as budgeting, analyzing statistics, and understanding probabilities.

Mathematics encompasses an extensive and complex landscape, beginning with essential elements and advancing into higher-level domains. Here is an outline of its hierarchy, emphasizing arithmetical reasoning and extending across various fields. Mathematics education follows a systematic approach, starting with fundamental concepts and progressing to more sophisticated structures of thought. As students' comprehension deepens, they are equipped to tackle increasingly challenging problems.

Here is a summary of mathematics from grades K through around 10th grade:

- Basic arithmetic: Addition, subtraction, multiplication, and division.
- Place value, number sense, and understanding decimals.
- Fractions, percentages, and ratios.
- Basic geometry: Shapes, angles, and measurement.
- Order of operations and simple expressions.
- Understanding variables and solving basic equations.
- Exponents, powers, and roots.

Our exploration of science and math is no more than arithmetic up to basic geometry, and as you see it comes early in our educations. Long before the advent of modern numeracy, now commonly called mathematics, numbers were regarded as sacred—they were the invisible scaffolding upon which reality itself was hung.

Ancient priest-astronomers understood number not merely as a tool for measurement but as a language of *divine architecture*. The language of numbers was enlarged to include the *qualities of the thing itself* that was being measured or counted, not limited to *quantities,* the counting of things. When both quantity and quality are taken together it brings us to think more deeply about the type of each thing being measured. That is what ancient sages pondered about, **it's the design or archetype of the thing itself** that's important to understand.

Number as Archetype

An *archetype* refers to the inherent, symbolic quality or essence of a number, beyond its quantitative value. Each number was believed to embody a distinct metaphysical principle or universal pattern, reflecting cosmic order and spiritual truth.

For example, "One" symbolized unity and origin; "Two," duality and polarity; "Three," harmony and synthesis. These numerical archetypes served as foundational templates in sacred geometry, where **archetypes encoded meaning into the structure of reality**, guiding interpretations of creation, consciousness, and the divine blueprint governing the universe and human soul alike.

Each number carried meaning, symbolic characteristics or resonance:

- **One (1)**: Unity, origin, like a seed, the monad.
- **Two (2)**: Duality, balance, polarity in opposites, the duad.
- **Three (3)**: Harmony, creation as a three-note chord, a triad.
- **Four (4)**: Materiality, foundation, the tetrad.
- **Nine (9)**: Completion, wholeness, the return to unity.

These symbolic associations were used to encode cosmology into temples, texts, and timekeeping systems. Symbolic opposites were often employed in ancient philosophy to represent broader metaphysical concepts, such as right and left, male and female, light and darkness. These were not arbitrary but reflected religious and cosmological principles—purity versus impurity, life versus death.

Philosophers like Pythagoras and Plato used these oppositions to explore ethics, reality, and the nature of the soul. For Pythagoras, numbers were more than quantity—they were the elemental patterns of harmony in both music and everything in the cosmos.

Where did these ideas originate?

74

Pythagorean Number Theory

The Pythagorean school viewed mathematics as a spiritual discipline. The **tetractys**—a triangular pattern of the first four numbers (1 + 2 + 3 + 4 = 10)—was held sacred, representing the harmony of the cosmos and the basis of musical intervals.

They discovered that musical harmony could be reduced to simple ratios between vibrating strings:

- **Octave** = 2:1
- **Fifth** = 3:2
- **Fourth** = 4:3

These same ratios later appeared in orbital mechanics, atomic structure, and biological systems.

Ratios Across Nature:

- **Orbital Mechanics**: Kepler's third law shows that orbital periods and distances exhibit harmonic relationships.
- **Planetary Distances**: Titius-Bode law suggests geometric patterns.
- **Periodic Table**: Atomic weights and electron configurations reflect ratios and periodicity.

Thus, ratios are not arbitrary, they mirror the interconnected order of the physical world.

A Table of Elemental Forms

The **Periodic Table** is a remarkable scientific achievement that organizes elements based on their atomic number, electron configurations, and recurring chemical properties. This is an example of structure of thought, as it was with eyes wide open, that I first looked at a periodic table in high school chemistry class hanging high above the teacher's desk and podium.

Reflecting on my chemistry class, my understanding of matter has evolved significantly beyond just *the elements*. One must consider that everything comes into existence through structured thought. Atoms, which appear as lifeless "elements" on the chart, might be organized intelligence. These atoms function as building blocks, forming molecules and progressively more complex organic compounds. To understand this, one must be a diligent student, observing the consistent patterns present in all things. These patterns are both physically and mentally connected at the sub-atomic level, where periodic movements give rise to substances.

The origin of the word "periodic" can be traced back to the Greek term *periodos*, which means "a going around" or "cycle." Over time, the term evolved to signify "recurring at regular intervals" in English. Additionally, **periodicity is akin to frequency**, which is measured in cycles per second as a rate of occurrence, a concept that will be discussed further in our review.

Here's a brief history:

- **Early Groupings**: In 1789, Antoine Lavoisier classified elements as metals and nonmetals. Later, Johann Döbereiner **identified "triads" of elements** with similar properties. (remember the term: triads)
- **Law of Octaves**: In 1864, John Newlands proposed that every eighth element shared similar properties, likening it to **musical octaves**. He saw harmony in the elements of chemistry.
- **Mendeleev's Breakthrough (1869)**: Dmitri Mendeleev created the first widely recognized periodic table, arranging elements by atomic weight and leaving gaps for undiscovered ones. He predicted the properties of elements like Gallium and Germanium before their discovery.
- **Modern Refinements**: Henry Moseley (1913) reorganized the table by atomic number, resolving inconsistencies. Quantum mechanics later explained electron configurations and periodicity.

The periodic table displays the organization of the physical world, illustrating how atomic weights and electron configurations reveal systematic patterns and ratios. As scientific knowledge advances, it becomes clear that everything in the physical world, including biological life, consists of elements listed on the periodic table. Life exists due to the presence of energy.

Biological life evolved through combinations of elements to produce complex organisms, and the elements that comprise our bodies function within a broad network of periodic and cyclical systems. These are concepts derived in metaphysics and biology—later in this discourse, we must address theological beliefs about the creation. But first let's develop a historical perspective, then move into other topics that expand our methods for acquiring knowledge.

Number Systems of Antiquity

Ancient civilizations developed numerical systems tailored to cosmic and architectural harmony:

- **Babylonian Base-60**: known as the **sexagesimal system**, was a numeral system developed by the ancient Babylonians around 3100 BCE. It is one of the earliest known positional numeral systems and has had a lasting impact on modern mathematics and timekeeping. The system used 60 as its base, meaning numbers were expressed in powers of 60. The number 60 is highly divisible, with factors including 1, 2, 3, 4, 5, 6, 10, 12, 15, 20, 30, and 60. This made calculations involving fractions much simpler.
  1. **Timekeeping**: The division of an hour into 60 minutes and a minute into 60 seconds originates from this system.
  2. **Geometry**: The 360 degrees in a circle also stem from the base-60 system.

3. **Astronomy**: Babylonians used the system for astronomical calculations, which were remarkably advanced for their time
- **Vedic Base-12/360**: Embodies a mathematically elegant and symbolically rich approach to measuring time, space, and cosmological order. It reflects the deep harmonics of ancient Indian cosmology, embedding astronomical and spiritual truths into its structure. This number system, with its emphasis on **harmonic resonance, divisibility**, and **sacred geometry**, forms the basis of much Vedic thought and practice and remains influential in modern metaphysical and alternative scientific circles This numerical framework found in ancient Indian cosmology and metaphysics is intimately tied to Vedic timekeeping, astronomy, ritual practice, and cosmological models.
   1. The system blends a **duodecimal (base-12)** and
   2. Sexagesimal (base-60) structure,
   3. Culminating in a **360° circle**, widely seen in calendaring and astronomical applications.
- **Mayan Base-20**: A mathematically advanced, symbolically rich framework that integrated arithmetic, calendar science, and cosmology. With its efficient positional notation, early use of zero, and adaptation for calendrical precision, it rivals other ancient systems in sophistication. It offers a profound example of how numeracy, symbolism, and astronomy were fused to interpret time and the cosmos—revealing a mathematically encoded worldview based on harmony, recurrence, and celestial observation.
   1. **Zero Concept**: Maya independently developed a concept of **zero**. Used as a **placeholder** in positional notation, which allowed true arithmetical operations.

2. **Calendar and Astronomy:** Tracked vast cycles of time, essential for prophecy and ritual.
3. **Ecliptic calculations, Venus cycles, and solar/lunar eclipses:** Predicted using mathematical tables carved in stone and painted in codices

- **Egyptian Sacred Cubits**: Represents a unification of **mathematics, cosmology, and spiritual architecture**. More than a measuring rod, it embodies harmonic principles encoded in both physical structures and metaphysical beliefs. Its precise use in the layout of temples and pyramids reflects a worldview in which architecture is a mirror of the cosmos.

Each of these ancient systems reflected harmonic coherence with the stars, sun, and seasons. **Babylonian system** was replaced by the decimal system in most contexts; however, its influence persists in how we measure time, angles, and geographic coordinates.

Number in Metaphysics and Geometry

Plato's contributions to metaphysics and geometry are profound and enduring, shaping Western thought and mathematics for centuries.

Here's a brief overview:
Metaphysics
1. **Theory of Forms**: Plato proposed that the material world is a shadow of a higher, unchanging realm of ideal forms. These forms represent perfect, eternal truths, such as the concept of beauty or justice, and are accessible through reason rather than sensory experience.
2. **Dualism**: He introduced the idea of a dualistic reality, dividing existence into the world of forms, and the

physical world, influencing later philosophical and theological thought.

3. **Mathematical Idealism**: Plato viewed numbers and geometric shapes as existing in the realm of forms, representing perfect, immutable truths.

Geometry

1. **Platonic Solids**: Plato explored the five regular polyhedra—tetrahedron, cube, octahedron, dodecahedron, and icosahedron—now known as Platonic solids. He associated these shapes with the classical elements and the cosmos.

2. **Geometry as a Gateway**: He emphasized the importance of geometry in understanding the universe, famously inscribing "Let no one ignorant of geometry enter here" at the entrance of his Academy.

3. **Foundation for the Quadrivium**: Plato's Academy laid the groundwork for the study of four key branches of knowledge: arithmetic, geometry, astronomy and music. These were collectively known as the quadrivium, which became central to classical education.

Plato's integration of metaphysical concepts with mathematical reasoning continues to inspire discussions on the nature of reality and the role of abstract thought. Many aspects of his legacy resonate with the ideas in spirit science.

Plato taught that geometry was the divine language. Numbers became embodied in shapes:

- **Triangle (3)**: Dynamic stability
- **Square (4)**: Order and material balance
- **Pentagon (5)**: Life and phi ratio

The golden ratio (ϕ) and square roots (e.g., $\sqrt{2}$) structured how parts relate to wholes. This sacred geometry governed the design and form of temples, art, and now we see spirals of DNA that resonate with geometric design.

Digital Roots and Esoteric Codes

Ancient numerologists reduced large numbers to **digital roots** by summing their digits repeatedly until a single digit remained. This MOD(9) arithmetic revealed harmonic consistencies:

- $432 \rightarrow 4 + 3 + 2 = 9$
- 108 (sacred in Vedic culture) $\rightarrow 1 + 0 + 8 = 9$

The recurrence of the number 9 in ancient sacred numbers suggests a cycle of resonance embedded in all of reality. Humans are also part of this physical reality, existing in harmonic resonance, which connects us to the mental universe. Consciousness is considered a part of creation, and humans participate in the ongoing process of creation.

Zecharia Sitchin: Ancient Astronaut Theorist and Interpreter of the Sumerian Past

1. Narrative Overview

Zecharia Sitchin (1920–2010) was an author, linguist, and independent researcher best known for his controversial ancient astronaut theory and the series *The Earth Chronicles*. Born in Azerbaijan and educated in Mandatory Palestine and the United Kingdom, Sitchin studied ancient languages, including Sumerian cuneiform, and developed a fascination with Mesopotamian texts and mythologies.

Sitchin gained prominence with the 1976 publication of *The 12th Planet*, where he argued that ancient Sumerian records describe extraterrestrial beings called the Anunnaki. According to Sitchin, these beings came from a distant, yet-undiscovered planet beyond Neptune—named Nibiru—and genetically engineered early humans as a slave race to mine gold. He interpreted Mesopotamian mythology and biblical texts as literal accounts of ancient contact between humans and advanced alien visitors.

His works, blending ancient history with astronomy and genetic engineering, gained a global following and influenced the development of modern ancient astronaut theory alongside figures like Erich von Däniken. Despite lacking academic credentials in archaeology or Assyriology, Sachin's books have sold millions of copies and remain popular in alternative history circles.

2. Most Important Contributions
- Author of The Earth Chronicles series, starting with The 12th Planet
- Popularization of the ancient astronaut theory using Sumerian texts
- Fusion of myth, astronomy, and speculative archaeology
- Provocation of debate around early human origins and ancient cosmology

3. Disbelief and Skepticism
Mainstream historians, linguists, and archaeologists have widely criticized Sitchin's interpretations, pointing to mistranslations and speculative leaps. His theories are generally classified as pseudoscience or fringe archaeology.

4. Restated Key Contributions
Sitchin reawakened public fascination with Sumerian mythology by reinterpreting it through the lens of space exploration and extraterrestrial contact. His narrative framework brought ancient stories into contemporary mythmaking.

5. Lessons for Readers
- Alternative narratives can inspire curiosity about ancient history.
- Popular science and mythology often blur lines to provoke new questions.
- Interpretation of ancient texts shapes cultural understanding.
- Fringe theories, while often unsupported, can ignite mainstream reevaluation.
- Truth-seeking requires both imagination and rigorous methodology.

Conclusion—Sentient Machines

Some readers may question the relevance of ancient technology in our advanced modern world, especially considering the widespread illiteracy of past eras. It is advisable not to dismiss its importance without first gathering sufficient evidence of its significance in the 21st century. There are scholars that have discovered evidence that **non-human entities** contributed to a vast advancement of human knowledge. Empires have risen and fallen many times, and hidden knowledge that was lost comes around again, pounding against tidal waves of ignorance.

"The more we learn, the less certainty we find to entertain ourselves."—Elmo

---

With the aid of non-human entities, and their influences, those who became educated did not want to freely share everything they were taught. They formed small enclaves with only a few trusted people within their circle of influence and secret societies were formed to protect the libraries consisting of scrolls. **Secrets that were learned, or knowledge of events that have taken place, were closely guarded in the past, and openly revealed herein. Economic power and social status are naturally occurring human motivations. It occurs that the best way to keep secrets is to write (publish) on scrolls and hide them.**

How did ancient philosophers know so much about the cosmos, when many believed the world was flat?

The following chapters will present various insights. This book suggests that as you continue reading, you may encounter breakthroughs that were not initially apparent. Persistence may lead to discoveries, and there are many ancient facts unknown to modern sciences. This is due to the·

way knowledge has been compartmentalized rather than integrated into a broad understanding.

Scholars often regard ancient metaphysical and philosophical domains with skepticism, considering ancient history to be mythological rather than based on evidence. Imagine how the evolution of artificial intelligence becomes a sentient self-aware machine—how will it view the typical human? That future may have already arrived unbeknownst to many—as you are reading this, after its publication, whilst I was carefully studying the rate of progress in AI.

Does this include you? Apologies, I diverged from what I should focus on—revealing the truth.

To scholars in ancient cultures, numbers were not contrived or invented; they were discovered through thoughtful reflection. The significance of each number is that it bore a vibrational essence and cosmological power. As we step into harmonic cosmology, we carry forward this sacred understanding: that numbers are not just quantities but reveal vibrational qualities. The cosmos is not random but a resounding symphony of numerical songs waiting to be heard.

A Universe of Vibrations

Light is like a sound that vibrates along on the electromagnetic spectrum at wavelengths that we see—vibrating the optic nerves giving information to our brains. Sounds come to our cognition and perception, as audible signals that vibrate the nerves inside our ears. It's the quality of the medium that differentiates these frequencies—coming into our perceptions. Air resonates with the sound waves that reach our ears. Light travels through the vacuum of empty space, but as it highlights the atmosphere, a rainbow might appear.

The cosmos is not a chaotic, disconnected void but rather a grand, harmonious symphony of interconnected patterns and rhythms. Numbers form the essence of this universal musical language unspoken yet deeply revealing itself, yearning to be understood through every layer of

84

existence. Our minds and bodies cannot be separated from the cosmos and are subject to nature's orderly laws and its formations are evidenced through numbers.

From the precise orbit of planetary bodies to the delicate arrangement of subatomic particles, a masterpiece is revealed in mathematics which serves as its unifying score. Every phenomenon, from the spiraling dance of galaxies to the vibrational frequencies of the atoms within us, is guided by numerical ratios and geometrical symmetry.

Fibonacci sequences that lead to golden ratios—these are but fragments of the celestial melodies echoing across the vastness of space and time. Fibonacci sequences describe biological and celestial energy flow and growth into spiral geometries of DNA—life forms are made from the architecture defined within their DNA inscriptions. All these living things are harmonized to each other and this planet upon which earthlings' dwell.

Earth's Heartbeat

The Schumann resonance is essentially the pulse or heartbeat of the earth. (see: Harmonics of Thought) Our pursuit of knowledge is at first to pour a solid foundation and then extend our realm into an understanding of how our conscious awareness develops human capabilities to become supernatural individually and collectively. The power of collective work brings us exponential growth for societal empowerment and brings forth global changes.

Early in life, I felt pressure to follow certain expectations, but eventually I learned to think independently, and I discovered a life filled with purpose. Discerning architecture of consciousness helped me to make clear, confident decisions—even when others doubted me.

From the philosophical clash between religion and science, we shift our focus toward the subtle frequencies and resonances that govern thought itself. Beyond doctrines and disciplines lies a deeper, more nuanced landscape, the harmonic architecture of the mind. In the following chapter, we examine how thought functions not just as cognition, but as vibration, creating the very fabric of our emotional and spiritual experience.

Chapter 4: Harmonics of Thought

Introduction—Life is Vibrational

Music is a universal language, composed of patterns of vibration and resonance, and intriguingly, so too is thought. As Albert Einstein once mused, "Everything in life is vibration." Our thoughts, like the notes in a symphony, carry specific frequencies and harmonics that shape the flow of mental energy. These rhythms influence not only our emotional states but also the coherence of how we perceive and interact with the world.

"If you want to find the secrets of the universe, think in terms of energy, frequency, and vibration."— Nikola Tesla

---

When our thoughts align harmoniously—clear, focused, and emotionally balanced—they create a resonance within us that extends outward, shaping the experiences we attract. As Nikola Tesla suggested, understanding the universe means thinking in terms of energy, frequency, and vibration. This principle underpins the power of human thought: a dynamic interplay of neural patterns vibrating in synchrony.

Our ancient philosopher **Pythagoras believed in the "music of the spheres,"** positing that celestial bodies emit vibrations that reflect cosmic harmony. Similarly, our minds echo this universal order, drawing strength from resonant, positive thoughts. **When mental patterns fall into dissonance—scattered, conflicted, or unaligned— they disrupt our inner rhythm, creating chaos in perception and intent.** By nurturing thoughts that vibrate at higher frequencies, we align ourselves with the fundamental harmonics of life, fostering clarity, well-being, and a deeper connection to the universe.

HARMONICS OF THE UNIVERSE

BODY   SOUL

Musical Ratios in the Cosmos

From the vibration of a string on a violin to the rotation of a planet, the laws of harmony govern the architecture of the universe. These laws are not arbitrary; they are rooted in mathematics, sound, and the resonant interplay of proportion. **Musical ratios**, long studied by ancient cultures, provide insight into how **space and form may be structured by vibrational mathematics**.

The Monochord and Harmonic Discovery

Pythagoras used the **monochord**, a single-stringed instrument, to explore how dividing a string produced distinct musical intervals:

- Dividing by **1:2** yielded an **octave**
- Dividing by **2:3** gave a **perfect fifth**
- Dividing by **3:4** created a **perfect fourth**

These foundational ratios are a part of the Western musical scale and extend beyond music to the design of temples, orbits, and timekeeping systems in ancient and contemporary times.

The Harmonic Series and Natural Resonance

The harmonic series is a progression of, **f multiples**, **frequencies**:

- f, 2f, 3f, 4f, ...

Each overtone is a multiple of a fundamental tone, forming **consonant blends**. In cosmology, this principal echoes in the **spacing of planetary orbits** and **celestial harmonics**.

Celestial Intervals Bring Planets into Harmony

Plato described the cosmos as a divine instrument tuned by a cosmic artisan. **Kepler**, in *Harmonices Mundi* (1619), calculated musical intervals between planetary motions:

- Mercury and Earth = Major Third
- **Earth and Venus** = Approx. Perfect Fifth

These weren't metaphors. Ancient thinkers believed the heavens emitted a kind of **silent music**, unheard, yet measurable through geometry and time. The universe is in a constant state of vibration, producing sounds characterized by specific ratios and frequencies. By examining musical intervals, we can identify correlations between sound and structure, as well as resonance and reality. Ancient civilizations correctly understood that the cosmos operates in harmony, and through harmonic cosmology, modern science is rediscovering this concept.

Musicians must quickly learn the importance of tuning instruments to achieve harmony within an ensemble. Similarly, we must align our mental frequencies with the earth's natural frequency to maintain our physical wellbeing in harmony with nature. Life is driven by harmonic vibrations that continuously flow through us, and it is essential to allow these vital energies uninterrupted passage.

Harmonic Ratios in Planetary Distances

- Earth–Moon ratio ≈ **3.67:1** → Close to a **perfect fourth**
- Sun:Earth diameter ≈ **109:1** → Close to **9 × 12.1**, suggesting octave cycles
- Earth–Sun:Earth–Moon distance ≈ **389:1** → Similar to harmonic resonances in fifth cycles

These ratios reveal a **symphonic consistency** in celestial dimensions.

Ancient Musical Tuning Systems and Cosmology

- **Pythagorean Tuning**: Built from perfect fifths (3:2)
- **Just Intonation**: Used 5:4 and 6:5 for major/minor thirds

Temples like the **Great Pyramid** are thought to amplify harmonic frequencies. Ancient builders embedded these ratios into stone, preserving cosmic music in sacred architecture.

Vibration, Cymatics, and Spatial Patterning

Cymatics: the study of visible sound through vibrating media (e.g., plates, fluids)

- **3:2 frequencies** → Hexagonal patterns
- **4:3 ratios** → Square and cross patterns

These patterns suggest that **vibrational ratios shape not only sound but matter**, including biological forms and galactic spirals.

Universal Resonance and Frequency Architecture

- **Brainwaves**: Alpha ~8 Hz → Harmonic of Earth's Schumann resonance
- **Light spectra, atomic orbitals**, and **quantum fields** obey principles of vibrational spacing

This suggests that **the structure of space is harmonic**, not random. Matter and consciousness may align through these resonant principles. Space may be the "Final Frontier", but the earth is our home, and just as harmony is embedded in the design of our solar system, planet earth resonates with its own frequency.

Winfried Otto Schumann: Discoverer of Earth's Resonant Frequency

1. Narrative Overview

Winfried Otto Schumann (1888–1974) was a German physicist and professor who discovered a fundamental natural phenomenon now known as the Schumann resonance—an extremely low-frequency (ELF) electromagnetic pulse that vibrates in the space between Earth's surface and the ionosphere. Born in Tubingen, Germany, Schumann studied electrical engineering and physics during a time of great innovation in electromagnetism and atmospheric science.

While working at the Technical University of Munich, Schumann mathematically predicted that the Earth's atmosphere acts as a resonant cavity for electromagnetic waves. In 1952, using Maxwell's equations, he showed that lightning discharges around the globe generate electromagnetic waves that resonate in this cavity, typically at a frequency of around 7.83 Hz—what is now commonly referred to as the Earth's "heartbeat."

Though initially a theoretical finding, Schumann's predictions were confirmed by later empirical measurements and have since become a cornerstone in geophysics and space weather research. The Schumann resonance has also garnered interest in the fields of chronobiology and holistic medicine, where it is associated (controversially) with human brainwave frequencies, particularly the alpha wave band.

2. Most Important Contributions
- Mathematic prediction and confirmation of the Schumann resonance
- Advancements in the understanding of Earth's electromagnetic environment

- Contributions to electrodynamics and atmospheric physics

3. Disbelief and Skepticism

At the time, the idea of a planetary electromagnetic resonance was novel and largely ignored outside specialized physics circles. Only with technological advancements did the phenomenon gain broader scientific acceptance.

4. Restated Key Contributions

Schumann uncovered the Earth's resonant electromagnetic frequency, linking planetary-scale phenomena with fundamental physics. His work bridged theoretical physics and atmospheric science.

5. Lessons for Readers
- Even obscure theoretical work can have lasting global relevance.
- The Earth itself is a dynamic, vibrating system.
- Natural frequencies may play a larger role in biology than once believed.
- Innovation often precedes recognition.
- Basic scientific curiosity can uncover universal principles hidden in plain sight.

The universe vibrates and is never silent, it rings like a bell and sings out in **ratios and frequencies**. Through musical intervals, we uncover bridges between sound and structure, resonance and reality. The ancients were not mistaken: **the cosmos is tuned**, and through harmonic cosmology, we are learning to hear it once more. As a young music student, I was taught that we must tune our instruments to play in harmony with the rest of the band. This is true of our minds also, we must tune our mental frequency with the earth's natural frequency and that helps to keep our bodies in tune with nature. Life is the result of harmonic vibrations that pass through us continuously, and we cannot impede those life-giving energies.

The Power of Internal Coherence

When we live in alignment with our deepest values and purposes, we achieve what heart-brain science calls coherence—a physiological and psychological state in which the rhythms of the heart, brain, and nervous system synchronize. This coherence can be measured through heart rate variability and is linked to greater emotional stability, resilience, and cognitive function. To awaken to our supernatural potential, we must attune not only our thoughts but the very frequencies that shape our being.

Coherence is not accidental. It arises from intentional practices like—breath regulation, focused attention, and elevated emotions such as gratitude, love or compassion. These practices tune our inner frequency, allowing us to resonate emotions into higher-order patterns in nature and society. Emotions are easily stimulated with sounds that bring happiness and harmony.

The Role of Emotional Energy

Thoughts and emotions are intimately connected. Emotions function as the fuel behind thought, driving actions—giving power and momentum to ideas. When emotional energy aligns with purpose, it catalyzes transformation. For example, a person who channels the emotions of gratitude and compassion into their daily interactions not only transforms their relationships but also reshapes their self-image and life path.

It is known that every emotional path leads to a unique experience for everyone. Listening to stories written by others and then adopting them as beliefs—whether from historical accounts or modern research studies—often cannot merge with the unique circumstances of individual experiences. Each person's likes, fears, wants, and motives are influenced by distinct experiences from relationships encountered from childhood onward into adulthood. Love is identified as a

93

creative emotion that brings people together to create new life—an electromagnetic force harmonizing the spirit within us.

Happiness, health, and well-being must originate from within each person's emotional expectations, beliefs and responses. Fear is caused by various factors and affects individuals differently, consistently being a destructive influence. It is considered an absolute truth that personal choices between creation or destruction are irrefutable. We create circumstances that help us to flourish, or those which help to destroy us. Happiness, health, and wealth are interconnected, and can be experienced both individually and in conjunction with society.

This feedback loop between thought, emotion, and identity is central to the blueprint of mind. When we consciously cultivate positive emotional energy—through gratitude, joy, love and hope—we accelerate personal evolution.

The Chemistry of Emotion – Insights from Candace Pert

In our expanding inquiry into the structured relationship between emotion and biological reality, it is essential to recognize the profound contribution of Dr. Candace B. Pert. Her work revolutionized our understanding of the emotional body, providing scientific grounding for what ancient traditions have long suggested: that the mind and body are not separate—but one interconnected network, with emotion as the courier.

Dr. Pert's groundbreaking book, *Molecules of Emotion: The Science Behind Mind-Body Medicine*, published in 1997, stands as a seminal text in the field of *psychoneuroimmunology*, the study of how thoughts and feelings influence neurological and immune function. Her discovery of the opiate receptor—the first receptor site ever identified on the surface of human cells—opened the door to a new paradigm: the body is not merely a passive recipient of chemical signals; it is an active participant in interpreting and responding to consciousness.

94

At the heart of Pert's thesis is the idea that emotions are not abstract psychological states—they are physical, measurable, and biologically encoded in the form of neuropeptides and their corresponding receptors. These molecules of emotion, as she called them, are released in response to our thoughts and feelings and travel throughout the body to regulate everything from mood to immunity.

"The chemicals that are running our body and our brain are the same chemicals that are involved in emotion." — Candace B. Pert

---

This revelation has extraordinary implications for the theory of structured thought. It affirms that emotions act as translators between our mental environment and our biological state. Our thoughts create an emotional response. Emotion triggers the release of specific hormones and neurochemicals. These molecules then influence our physiological systems, especially the immune system, endocrine, and nervous systems.

This cascade reinforces the model that thought precedes emotion, and emotion catalyzes biology. Thought → Emotion → Hormone → Behavior → Outcome. When this chain is governed by intentional, structured thought, we become the authors of our internal chemistry.

When we experience stress, for example, the hypothalamus releases corticotropin-releasing hormone (CRH), setting off a chain reaction that floods the body with cortisol and adrenaline. These substances are not inherently harmful—they are appropriate for acute danger—but when produced chronically through unstructured or negative thinking, they contribute to inflammation, immune suppression, and disease.

Fear is a biological trait found in natural living organisms. However, artificial intelligence does not experience fears that affect human and animal behaviors that promoted survival. Machine intelligence has been introduced to aid humans in various tasks, potentially leading to changes in our instinctive behaviors, yet persisting in the animal kingdom. Artificial intelligence cannot experience fear. Eliminating our thoughts about external danger, hunger, or other factors for survival will allow us to evolve beyond our past experiences, becoming more confident in our inner self.

Tools for Harmonic Alignment

- Binaural beat auditory rhythms.
- Breath training using simple paced deep breathing.
- Heart-focused meditation to amplify gratitude and compassion.
- 432 Hz music and binaural beats to shift brainwave activity.
- Daily affirmations are designed to synchronize intent with action.
- Journaling provides insight by decluttering the mind and noticing patterns.

Each tool presented in this book is a form of tuning—a way to adjust the harmonics of your thought matrix and bring your mental-emotional field into greater order. A poorly tuned instrument will ruin the sound of an orchestral performance. The human body cannot function properly until we eliminate mental distortions and bring our body into harmony with its design, which is controlled by our thoughts and emotions. These tools and techniques are proven and simple to use in realigning harmony within the internal systems of the body. To awaken to our supernatural potential, we must attune not only our thoughts but the very frequencies that shape our being.

Creative imagination is the tuning fork for consciousness. By aligning thought and intention with specific vibrational frequencies, we activate innate healing and cognitive potentials. Just as harmonic resonance can restore coherence in chaotic systems, our bodies and minds respond to purposeful vibrational entrainment. Entrainment means to stimulate our brainwaves with specific audible sounds that calm our mental states. Frequency tuning, such as attuning to 432Hz, aligns the biofield to cosmic harmonies, unlocking doorways to higher intuition and wellness.

What makes this global symphony truly extraordinary is its accessibility from humble individual efforts. Through the mindful pursuit of science, geometry, and philosophy, humanity can unravel the mystery of life revealing our true purpose—to expand consciousness—to express unlimited love—to create life. We have been able to hear and decode these numerical songs, revealing profound truths about our place in the universe.

This should serve to remind us that our existence is not arbitrary, and we are deeply interconnected—a reflection of universal order and purpose. Each of us must discover the unique purpose of our roles, then serve and further the creation. We are not merely observers listening to this symphony, we are also conductors playing our instruments, expressing notes and chords. Our thoughts, actions, and creations are expressions of the same underlying numerical harmony. By tuning ourselves to the frequency of the cosmos, we can align with its inherent order, finding clarity, connection, and meaning in the profound resonance of existence. Beneath the apparent chaos of existence lies a hidden order—an intelligent design guiding the dance of life.

Cosmic Law and Natural Order

The universe operates through immutable cosmic laws and natural order. From the orbit of galaxies to the beating of the human heart, harmony arises from adherence to these principles. Human prosperity, individually and collectively, depends on aligning thought, behavior, and creation with this grand architecture. Disregard for natural law leads to chaos and collapse; reverence for it leads to flourishing and evolution.

Natural law refers to the universal principles and inherent order that govern both the natural world and human experience. *It is the underlying set of truths—often considered self-evident—that operate regardless of human intervention or belief.* Gravity affects objects independent of personal beliefs. An example is when a person jumps from a height; they will experience the effects of gravity and learn about their body's weight.

While in elementary school, I was out on the playground. Out of curiosity, I jumped into a stairwell from a height of about 12-14 feet to the bottom landing; I quickly learned about gravity's impact, a lesson learned without incurring injury. Later, in my science class we were taught about the laws of gravity. No one taught me not to climb over that rail—that should have been self-evident.

A cannonball follows a predictable pathway if a known quantity of explosive charge propels a known weight of the cannonball forward. Isaac Newton described the Laws of Motion using formulas still in use today, enabling calculations of force and momentum to approximate the cannonball's travel distance. Soldiers have practiced aiming projectiles at targets since ancient times, such as during the Roman Empire, where catapults were used. Hollywood often portrays the laws of motion with remarkable accuracy.

These laws represent the blueprint by which the cosmos maintains harmony, balance, and growth. In applying the concept to our lives, natural law suggests that well-being and fulfillment arise when our thoughts, actions, and creations are aligned with these fundamental patterns of order. Just as musical harmony depends on the laws of acoustics, the harmony of the mind and society depends on our resonance with these timeless principles.

Understanding the harmonics of thought enhances our ability to comprehend the inner workings of our minds, leading to a deeper understanding of our cognitive processes. My father attended the Detroit Diesel School, a vocational training institute for mechanics. There, he learned the intricacies of engine operation, problem diagnosis, tool selection, and the execution of necessary repairs to ensure engines operated smoothly. He was proficient in maintaining optimal engine performance and tuning.

Cardboard Stethoscope

I was always impressed by dad's technique of using a cardboard tube from an empty paper towel roll as a stethoscope to listen to the *heart beats* of an engine during tuning. Initially, I did not grasp the purpose of this method, but it became evident that through harmonics, he could discern issues such as piston timing discrepancies or appreciate the harmonious functioning of an engine. He sought to identify the internal harmony within the engine block and its components. These principles have influenced my current understanding of the human mind, body, and thoughts, which can either be out of sync with nature or well-balanced, contributing to overall wellbeing.

Implications for Social Harmony

Just as individuals can become coherent, so too can families, communities, and even civilizations. Collective coherence emerges when people share common values, communicate with empathy, and align their actions toward a shared vision. Harmonic thought, when scaled, becomes social resonance. It inspires cooperation, reduces conflict, and increases collective intelligence.

Imagine educational systems built not just on test scores but on cultivating coherence and creativity. Picture governance systems that prioritize ethical clarity and compassion. Harmonics of thought become a foundation for conscious civilization—a step toward becoming truly supernatural in the age of AI.

Conclusion

Having explored the vibrational and energetic nature of thought, we now delve into how these mental harmonics shape the very structure of our self-identity. The next chapter introduces the "*Blueprint of Mind*"—the subconscious architecture that governs behavior, perception, and growth. Understanding this inner scaffolding is key to rewriting our personal narratives and unlocking latent human potential.

Chapter 5: Blueprint of Mind

Introduction—The Evolution of Self

We each carry a ***blueprint of mind that's a foundational set of memories, beliefs, and mental models*** that shape how we interpret experience. While these original blueprints are formed in childhood, they are not fixed. Through reflection, intention, and practice, we become architects and revise our design more empowering mental landscapes—we draw a new blueprint using our imagination and cognitive abilities. However, the ink will be fresh, and the new blueprint gets finalized trough many repetitions, rewriting our mental pathways with new footprints that become embedded into the subconscious mind.

Personal Story: The Day the World Changed My Identity

A Birthday That Marked a New Identity

It was Sunday, and I awoke in Birmingham, Alabama, expecting to celebrate another birthday. However, the day did not bring the anticipated cake or festivities. Instead, we received news of a riot in our hometown of Detroit.

We were unable to return home due to the looting and arson that had overwhelmed the city. What should have been a joyful memory turned into a day of profound change. The innocence of childhood was replaced by an awareness of injustice, fear, and the breakdown of community order.

Upon our return, the devastation along Grand River Avenue was reminiscent of a war zone. Tanks and armed soldiers patrolled the streets I once knew well. S.S. Kresge, my preferred dime store, was reduced to a burnt-out shell.

That day, I lost not only a birthday celebration but also a part of my identity. I no longer felt merely like a proud

American; I became acutely aware that I was "a Black teenager from inner-city Detroit," navigating a world fraught with racial tension. It was the first time I realized how external events could drastically alter everything. My perception of America—and my household shifted fundamentally. I had to confront my racial identity and understand firsthand how societal forces and systemic injustice could strip away a child's innocence in an instant.

That moment forged the deeper questions that would animate my spiritual and intellectual journey. The riot didn't just rupture the soul of a city; it shattered my illusions of unity and fairness. These early traumas laid the foundation for questioning both social and societal narratives.

This was one of many experiences that ignited my search for a new framework of understanding—a pathway that would eventually lead me to the synthesis of science, consciousness, and spiritual truth. And most importantly, the ability to not simply tolerate the environment that surrounded me, but to influence and control the blueprint within my soul and to extend my reach within the community and the world.

The blueprint is the foundation for all habits or deliberate changes within our core personality. From it, we derive a unique identity, one possibility among all others, with a singular set of experiences that drives our sense of purpose. By becoming an expert architect, we learn how to tame and control the monkey inside our brain, and then we evolve into more capable versions of ourselves. But first, let's dive into the evolutionary history of human cognition, and more about when and how humans developed the awareness that separated us from the animal kingdom.

Storytellers—A Revolution in Cognitive Ability

The Cognitive Revolution, as described by Yuval Noah Harari in Sapiens, marks a pivotal moment in human history— roughly 70,000 years ago—when Homo sapiens developed the ability to think in abstract terms, communicate simple notions at first, to gradually to create shared myths, and then more complex ideas. This revolution was not about physical evolution but rather a leap in cognitive abilities that allowed humans to cooperate in large numbers, something no other species had achieved on such a scale.

Harari argues that this newfound ability to imagine and believe in things that do not exist—such as gods, nations, money, and laws—enabled Homo sapiens to organize societies beyond small tribal groups. Unlike other animals, which rely on direct communication and instinct, humans could now build collective identities and institutions based on shared beliefs. This ability to create and sustain fictional narratives gave rise to religion, trade, and political systems, shaping the trajectory of human civilization.

One of the most fascinating aspects of the Cognitive Revolution is its role in Homo sapiens' dominance over other human species, such as Neanderthals. While Neanderthals were physically stronger, they lacked the ability to form large, flexible social structures based on shared myths, which ultimately gave sapiens the upper hand. This revolution also led to rapid advancements in technology, art, and culture, setting the stage for the Agricultural and Scientific Revolutions that followed.

In essence, the Cognitive Revolution was the moment when humans became storytellers, dreamers, and architects of imagined realities, an ability that continues to define our species today. More to the observations that come alongside this are the implications of that conscious awareness of self, coincided with the ability to come together both in groups and individually, as self-identity aroused community.

Cognitive Senses

Humans indeed have cognitive abilities, allowing imagination and rational thought to guide our dominion over the Earth. Yet our perceptions are inherently limited, grounded in basic sensory experiences such as sight, smell, taste, hearing, and touch. Animals often surpass us in

103

sensory precision: dogs detect scents invisible to us, and cats navigate effortlessly in low-light environments. A multitude of creatures thrive using senses beyond our natural capabilities or knowledge.

Scientific inquiry highlights these perceptual limits but also empowers us to surpass them. Through innovation, we have created tools and technologies that significantly extend our sensory reach. As our instruments improve, our understanding of the universe deepens. Perhaps one day, these cumulative advancements will enable the universe to fully unveil its truths to humanity. Ultimately, we come face to face with the realities of our universe perfect detail, such that someday we might understand the whole truth.

Understanding Your Cognitive Blueprint

Consciousness is an architect that dreams of intelligent designs and a blueprint emerges. The blueprint of mind includes both conscious and subconscious elements. Consciously, we choose goals, form opinions, and make judgments. Subconsciously, our beliefs, biases, and emotional patterns guide much of our behavior. The more aware we become of our inner architecture; the more power we acquire to change ourselves and the environment.

"Man is not what he thinks he is, he is what he hides." — André Malraux

---

Our subconscious mind is the storage space where the soul is hidden away from conscious awareness. We can reprogram it; **neuroscience confirms that the brain stays adaptable throughout life—a phenomenon known as neuroplasticity.** Thoughts, repeated over time, physically alter the structure of neural pathways. This means transformation is not only psychological—it is biological.

Mental Cognition System

The Mental Cognition System can be conceptualized as the processes and mechanisms by which the mind acquires, processes, stores, and uses information. And again we find an example of duality, another two-fold pattern has emerged from unity, embedded into our mental software.

It consists of two layers that process and hold information:

- Conscious Mind
  a. Processing of non-threating information
  b. Reflecting on what's going on, putting it into context.
  c. Lessons from the past are recalled and considered.
  d. Decision-making occurs.
  e. Delegation of "learned experiences" to Subconscious mind
- Subconscious Mind
  a. Holds emotional triggers
  b. Frightening or unforgettable experiences
  c. Quickly reacts without higher conscious thought.
  d. Fight or Flight

Here's a breakdown of our cognitive blueprint, its components, and their functions:

1. Sensory Input:
   a. *Sensory organs* gather physical **signals intelligence** from the environment:
      i. sight
      ii. auditory/hearing
      iii. sense of smell
      iv. sense of taste
      v. touch
   b. Information is collected and transmitted into the brain for processing.
2. Perception:

a. The brain interprets sensory information to form a coherent understanding of the environment.
b. Includes pattern recognition, object identification, and spatial awareness.
3. Attention:
   a. The cognitive process of selectively focusing on specific stimuli while ignoring others.
   b. Helps prioritize information for further processing.
4. Memory:
   a. Divided into multiple types:
      i. *Sensory Memory*: Brief storage of sensory information.
      ii. *Short-term/Working Memory*: Temporary storage and manipulation of information.
      iii. *Long-term Memory*: Durable storage of information, including explicit and implicit memories.
5. Learning and Decision Making:
   a. The process of acquiring new knowledge or skills.
   b. Involves modifying memory structures and creating new neural connections.
   c. Facilitating decision making by evaluating options.
   d. Choosing actions based on goals, values, and available information.
6. Reasoning and Problem-Solving:
   a. Logical processes that involve analyzing information, forming judgments, and solving complex problems.
7. Language and Communication:
   a. The ability to understand and produce language.

b. Essential for sharing thoughts, emotions, and ideas.
8. Emotional Regulation and Behavior:
   a. The influence of emotions on cognition, affecting attention, memory, and decision-making.
   b. Behavioral responses, including verbal communication, motor actions, or other observable outcomes.

The Conscious Mind

The conscious mind includes thoughts we are actively aware of—reasoning, planning, making decisions. **It operates slowly, deliberately, and governs voluntary action.** As we repeatedly make conscious decisions, they become firmly committed, thereby forming the subconscious mind.

"What comes to mind enters the brain, where thoughts are processed and stored. What comes out is anybody's guess, and that's everybody's problem."— Elmo

---

Subconscious response functions beneath awareness. It stores habits, emotional patterns, conditioned responses, and autonomic processes—such as the coordination of the sympathetic and parasympathetic systems. Mental components are a software-based command and control system.

Table 4.1

Table 4.1 - Mental Dualities	
Cognition System	Nervous System
1) Conscious Mind	1) Parasympathetic
2) Subconscious Mind	2) Sympathetic

This table shows the duality between the brain's cognitive and autonomic nervous systems, highlighting a core design principle. The mind functions like software while nerves act as hardware, transmitting signals and storing memories physically. Duality is observed widely in science and ancient numerology.

The Duality of Mind

We must distinguish between the *conscious mind* that is observant and creative and the *subconscious mind* that is habitual—*initially* programmed during childhood. Our intuitive **behavior is driven by the subconscious**, which can perpetuate self-limiting beliefs until reprogrammed. Our **beliefs function as filters** through which we interpret the world, and conscious interpretations create new signals that reshape us; causing changes in metabolism and cellular behavior throughout the body.

There are practical exercises described in later chapters, which give us control over both our software and hardware systems; through reprogramming the subconscious mind and taking greater control over the autonomic nervous system.

Autonomic Nervous System

The human nervous system is divided into **two primary branches within the autonomic system: the sympathetic and the parasympathetic nervous systems**. These subdivisions are a duality, and they function involuntarily, managing physiological states, typically without conscious effort. But through deliberate actions, we can acquire complete control.

The sympathetic nervous system is responsible for the "fight-or-flight" response—preparing the body for action by increasing heart rate, dilating pupils, releasing adrenaline, and redirecting blood flow to muscles.

In contrast, the parasympathetic nervous system governs the "rest-and-digest" state—slowing the heart rate, stimulating digestion, and conserving energy to maintain long-term equilibrium. These systems operate through networks of nerves branching from the spinal cord and brainstem to nearly every organ, responding reflexively to perceived internal and external conditions.

Above this neural landscape lies the **brain**, an integrated command center. The **brainstem** manages autonomic responses, while the **limbic system** oversees emotional processing, and the **prefrontal cortex** exercises executive control.

Conscious and Subconscious Mind

The conscious mind includes thoughts we are actively aware of—reasoning, planning, making decisions. It operates slowly, deliberately, and governs voluntary action.

The subconscious mind, however, functions beneath awareness. It stores habits, emotional patterns, conditioned responses, and autonomic processes—such as the coordination of the sympathetic and parasympathetic systems. The subconscious mind regulates the autonomic nervous system, which in turn regulates stress in the body. This is a very important concept that must be understood. Chronic stress is the root of many diseases, and we have the ability to lower our stress level with deliberate relaxation strategies.

These systems are deeply interconnected. Emotional stress, consciously perceived, can activate the sympathetic system to elevate stress, even in the absence of a physical threat. Conversely, deliberate breathing and mindfulness can stimulate the parasympathetic system, calming the body to signal safety.

The Hardware and Software Working Together

In essence, the nervous system serves as the body's hardware, while the mind functions as its software. The conscious mind has the capability to influence the subconscious, which, in turn, regulates the autonomic nervous system.

This interconnectedness underscores why structured thinking, mindfulness, and emotional regulation are essential tools for achieving optimal health and self-mastery. By understanding these relationships, individuals can deliberately shift their biological state—from stress to relaxation, and from reactive behavior to intentional responses—creating a foundation for profound transformation in mind, body, and spirit.

Why do we need a mind-to-body stress regulator?

The subconscious mind acts like a traffic controller, directing thoughts and emotions to calm or stimulate the nervous system. It functions as a mediator, converting recurring thoughts, emotions, and beliefs into physiological responses. **Emotions trigger the release of hormones like cortisol and adrenaline, which are natural and necessary under appropriate circumstances**. However, maintaining a constant state of stress should be avoided. Chronic anxiety, for instance, can keep the sympathetic nervous system overactive, negatively impacting overall health. Conversely, practices such as meditation can rewire these habitual responses. **Just twenty minutes of meditation daily can significantly reduce stress, illustrating the substantial benefits achievable through conscious mental practices.**

110

The Nervous System

In essence, the nervous system forms the body's hardware, while the brain and mind represent its software. **The conscious mind can *be trained to deliberately influence the subconscious, which in turn can regulate the autonomic nervous system*.** This interdependence explains why structured thought, mindfulness, and emotional regulation are vital for achieving optimal health and self-mastery. By understanding these systems, individuals can intentionally shift their biology—from stress to relaxation, from reactive to deliberately laying the groundwork for profound transformation of body, mind, and spirit.

The Evolution of Self

Ultimately, the blueprint of mind leads to the evolution of the self—that developed into personality traits—as we each observe one another to realize: "I Am". Selfhood is not a static state but rather an ongoing, dynamic process of transformation. Every day presents an opportunity to reshape our identity through deliberate thought and heightened emotional awareness. By engaging regularly in reflective practices aligned with the principles of conscious awareness, we transcend inherited patterns, outdated narratives, and societal conditioning. Thus, our mental blueprint becomes a living, adaptable guide—editable, continuously evolving, and empowering. We are able to command ourselves and to reflect an image of ourselves that empowers us through the mirror of our creative mind.

Looking In the Mirror at AI

In every age, humanity has faced the limits of its knowledge. The stars posed mysteries we could not yet solve; the microcosm of the atom revealed worlds within worlds. Each limit, when approached with humility and courage, became a threshold to a greater understanding. Likewise, AI presents not an end, but a mirror—reflecting both our genius and our fears. It asks: will we retreat into dependency and distraction, or will we rise into intentional creators of a new harmonic reality?

Becoming Supernatural in the Age of AI:

- Master the inner architecture of thought and feeling.
- Reclaim storytelling as a sacred and creative act— writing our own blueprint.
- Embrace science and spirituality not as opposites, but as complementary dimensions of a single unfolding reality.
- Foster love—the supreme creative force—as the guiding principle for personal and collective evolution.
- See artificial intelligence as the catalyst for humanity's spiritual maturity.

Conclusion

As we have explored, the blueprint of the mind profoundly shapes our personal evolution, influencing not only our perceptions but also our physical realities. Through conscious reflection, emotional coherence, and intentional action, we can harness neuroplasticity to rewrite our cognitive architecture, guiding ourselves toward a state of heightened awareness and well-being. This transformative process is not solely theoretical; it requires active engagement with structured thought patterns and disciplined emotional practices, facilitating deep, sustainable personal growth.

In the upcoming chapter, "Quantum Mindfulness and the New Human," we transition from the internal workings of individual transformation to broader insights that merge mindfulness with quantum field theory and principles. We will delve into how understanding quantum mechanics can further empower our consciousness, revealing new dimensions of human potential and connection. By aligning our internal coherence with the subtle quantum energies permeating our universe, we step closer to realizing the full spectrum of our supernatural capabilities, becoming active participants in shaping not only our own destinies but potentially influencing collective human evolution.

Chapter 6: Quantum Mindfulness

Introduction—The New Human

As humanity stands at the threshold of a technological and spiritual renaissance, a new paradigm emerges—one that fuses the wisdom of mindfulness with the insights of quantum physics. This synthesis, which we call quantum mindfulness, empowers individuals to access elevated states of awareness, influence subtle energies, and engage life with greater presence, intention, and compassion.

In the landscape of consciousness, truth endures beyond all temporal illusions, while ignorance withers under the light of awareness. Quantum mindfulness opens doors within our spirit that were closed to our physical abilities, where survival of the fittest was taught as essentially a means to an economic reward, where both intelligence and labor commitments are required of the self or from others.

This unveils a falsehood that cannot be sustained in the age of artificial intelligence that vastly exceeds human capacity. Yet in keeping with our wildest dreams, ignorance is dying as the golden age of machine intelligence emerges. Self-worth derived from perceived intellectual prowess is diminished as artificial intelligence exceeds human capabilities. Likewise, physical strength was diminished in the advent of gasoline engines.

We must educate ourselves on how artificial intelligence can support us in exploring new possibilities as our old economic structures are permanently transformed. This transformation paves the way for a new awareness and the emergence of a new human from the metaphorical darkness of our ancestral origins.

If you consider yourself to have achieved everything that you ever dreamed of becoming, then you are quite exceptional. Keep doing what you have always done. Otherwise, consider the possibility of being uninformed or unaware of what this means, i.e., ignorant of how supernatural power is attained. Keep reading!

The Mortality of Ignorance

Truth is everlasting; ignorance is fleeting. Beliefs based on falsehood inevitably collapse, while absolute truth, regardless of it seeming obscure, it persists across all time and generations. The pursuit of truth aligns with enduring principles of creation.

Unchallenged ignorance leads to deterioration and decline, as we are now facing. Humanity's future depends not merely on the accumulation of information but on the courageous pursuit of wisdom.

This treatise discusses the wisdom that propels humanity to its next stage in the evolutionary process, which is not about developing new physical attributes or enhancing physical strength. Instead, it focuses on surpassing survival tactics to become more humane and less harmful to other races, cultures, and the planet.

The More We Know

We have embarked upon a journey toward becoming supernatural beings. Now, the decisions before you are whether to continue, to persist or to contemplate alternative paths. It becomes evident that both limitations and boundlessness define our existence. Everyone's choice is personal and autonomous, as such, mutual respect for individual decisions is paramount.

The options presented herein involve either maintaining your normal routines of habitual existence, dog paddling in survival mode or soaring upward on a flight of the imagination. The process of redesigning and rewriting your new blueprint means passing through the gateway of transformation and achieving an enhanced state of being. These mental transactions are reversible, allowing us to be open-minded to every conceivable possibility.

Conscious Evolution and Quantum Mindfulness

Thus, the decision lies between—perpetuating a constant state of survival—or pursuing the transformative journey towards becoming supernatural. *The more we learn, the less we can predict—that is the paradox of the quantum mind.* The death of ignorance begets more questions and less steadfastness. No one can guarantee what the future holds, but when our intention is met with emotionally charged direction, everything and every pathway turns to our advantage—usually with unexpected surprises.

Physicists discovered that the universe's physical laws break down at the quantum level, leading to 100 years of investigation without a definitive theory or explanation. The combination of AI and quantum computer power will eventually inform us that consciousness within the universe is connected to our minds and passes through our thoughts to alter physical reality. Even after they found the evidence, disbelief has persisted.

Scientific beliefs are called laws because they were defined using the scientific method. However, they falsified those original *"laws"* through objective observations that led to an unpredictable outcome.

The Prospect of the Unpredictable

The famous "double-slit experiment" revealed that the behavior of waves and particles are unpredictable, because a person's thoughts during observations influence the outcome of the experiment. This proves that objective observations at the quantum level are impossible. Einstein called such phenomena "spooky," because they defied expectations, and showed that thoughts can unpredictably impact light photons, such that objective experiments became impossible. Photons are a wave/particle or the essence of light. The photon is the smallest measure of light emission.

The God Particle

Globally, physics labs are advancing quantum mechanics with massive investments, from CERN to Silicon Valley. The discovery and proof of the Higgs Boson (the "God Particle") adds a key piece toward the unified field theory—one of the potential theories that might someday explain everything. Useful applications remain elusive yet thought to be vital in getting beyond our current limitations.

Quantum computing research is dominated by companies like IBM, Microsoft, Google, Amazon, and several smaller firms, which are often bought by bigger names. In medicine, structural biology and MRI imaging are areas where quantum computing may lead to therapies replacing pharmaceuticals. Areas like quantum biology and healing are also being explored. Quantum computing addresses hardware requirements, due to the enormous processing speed, and AI solves complex problems using neural computing software and deep learning.

Understanding Quantum Mindfulness

Quantum mindfulness is the practice of consciously observing one's thoughts, feelings, and intentions as energetic phenomena. It draws from quantum theory, which recognizes that particles exist in potential states until observed, and from mindfulness traditions that emphasize nonjudgmental awareness of the present moment.

The Triad of Being—Body, Mind, and Soul

In the transformation from inert molecules to sentient beings, the structure of DNA alone cannot account for the mystery of life. The double helix contains instructions, but it does not initiate, build or animate the human form. Consciousness emerges not simply from biological substrates but from an intricate dance between physical structure, mental energy, and a deeper presence—the soul.

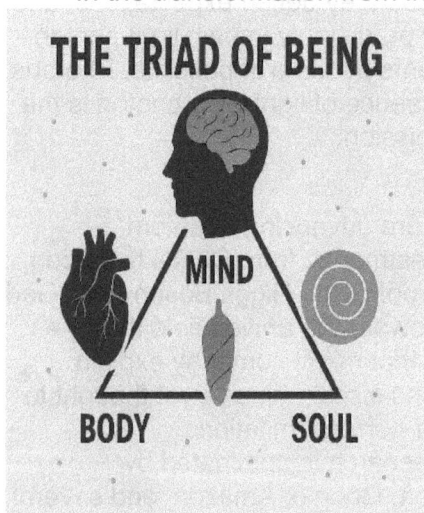

This threefold nature of existence—body, mind, and soul—is fundamental to the architecture of **Quantum Mindfulness**. It acknowledges that there is an initiating spark, a field of awareness that precedes cognition. The soul, in this model, is not an effect of biology but a causal force—the original note in the symphony of being that existed before and persists after life.

DNA provides the script, i.e., a blueprint for unique physical traits taken from the mother and father. Mind provides interpretation and memory of experiences. But the

118

soul—the animating witness—gives it purpose and direction. This balance of forces aligns with my Factor-9 cosmology: a harmonic model of emergence where three elements resonate together to create coherence, not chaos. When aligned, this triad unlocks a higher potential for human transformation—perhaps even evolution into what we now call "supernatural".

"The supernatural observer is not passive. In this mental model, the observer plays the role of active creator."—Elmo

---

Who are we as observers?

Human intellect continually raises profound questions about the universe—the number, distance, origin, and creation of stars—questions whose scale exceeds our observational and cognitive limits. Notwithstanding practical limits, our creative imagination is expressed through storytelling, and whether it is known as mythology, cosmology or science, we create something, entertain others and/or become more inspired. Acknowledging our inability to fully comprehend the universe's beginnings, purpose, or workings, we recognize our role as observers and narrators. Our primary function is capturing experiences and insights, preserving them through storytelling for future generations.

Storytelling arises from human cognition distinguishing us from other species. Our sense of curiosity and creativity get embedded into our observations and that changes physical reality. Our ability for reflection, imagination, and reasoning makes us fundamentally different from animals driven primarily by instinct. A crucial inquiry is whether our narratives originate from rational thought, imagination, superstition, or empirical evidence—questions that have deeply engaged my contemplation throughout life.

It is likely that we will arrive at new scientific evidence using artificial intelligence coupled with quantum computing to find the keys to an understanding of how consciousness affects or creates the physical realm. Our abilities to cause effects on physical matter through mental effort is no longer considered impossible, but increasingly likely, as we are becoming more supernatural, albeit rarely seen in the past. Religious teachings have always been about supernatural events being manifested—both in the past and to come again in the future.

The leading edge of science is leaning towards a story where thoughts initiate quantum events—a wave of potential collapsing into physical forms through focused attention and emotion—that become energetic. Thought has power to manifest into tangible observations. The more we cultivate clarity, stillness, and coherent emotional energy, the more powerfully we influence the probabilities of our future. My hypothesis is that consciousness exists everywhere, and functions in accordance with quantum mechanics. Quantum physics has proven that the inspector is not just an objective onlooker, but a projector aiming his/her own thought into the subject being inspected.

Practical Applications

Practicing quantum mindfulness involves the following core techniques:
- Present-state awareness through conscious breathing and sensory immersion
- Emotional regulation to maintain a stable, high-frequency state of being
- Visualization of desired quantum outcomes, held with focused intention
- Reframing disruptive or limiting beliefs in the moment of awareness

- Energetic hygiene, such as grounding and cleansing meditative practices

These practices strengthen the neural and energetic circuits responsible for conscious creation. Over time, practitioners notice a shift in their experiences—greater synchronicity, intuitive insight, and emotional resilience.

Beliefs or Genetic Determinism

"The moment you change your perception is the moment you rewrite the chemistry of your body." — Bruce H. Lipton

---

Overview of Dr. Bruce Lipton

Dr. Bruce H. Lipton, Ph.D., is a developmental biologist best known for his work in bridging science and spirituality through the emerging field of **epigenetics**, the study of how environmental systems affect gene expression. A former medical school professor and researcher at Stanford University's School of Medicine, Lipton gained widespread attention with the publication of his seminal book, *The Biology of Belief* (2005).

In our pursuit of understanding the nature of thought and its capacity to shape reality, one voice stands out in both its **scientific rigor and spiritual resonance—Dr. Bruce H. Lipton**. A former professor at Stanford University's School of Medicine and a pioneering biologist, Lipton has become widely recognized for his groundbreaking research in the field of epigenetics. *The Biology of Belief* **delivers a compelling case**: our thoughts, perceptions, and subconscious programming are not abstract or inconsequential; they are the literal architects of our biology.

These implications are vast. Lipton divides the mind into the conscious and the subconscious. The conscious mind is creative plans, aspires, and dreams. But the subconscious mind, programmed during early childhood, controls over 80-95% of our daily behavior. This automatic programming often contains outdated or self-limiting beliefs. Lipton shows that unless this subconscious script is restructured, even the most inspired conscious efforts will fail to overcome the programmed responses of fear, lack, or unworthiness.

This single sentence encapsulates a biological paradigm that affirms the deepest teachings of spiritual traditions: that healing, transformation, and personal evolution begin within. From the perspective of structured thought, **every affirmation, visualization, and moment of mindfulness is not merely a psychological activity, it is a biochemical one.**

Lipton's Contributions and Ideas

- Epigenetics Over Genetic Determinism--Lipton challenged the long-held belief that genes control biology in a fixed and deterministic way.
- He showed that the environment surrounding a cell, including energetic signals and perception, directly influences its behavior and gene activity.
- The Role of Perception and Belief: Lipton emphasized that the mind's perception—not the objective environment—is what controls biology.
- This implies that human beings are not victims of their genes, but active participants in shaping their biology.

The discovery of Dr. Bruce Lipton's research marked a turning point in my own journey of understanding the mind-body connection. His book challenged the very foundation of genetic determinism I was taught in college and totally believed. Where classical biology taught us, that DNA was our immutable destiny, Lipton presented evidence that **beliefs and feelings actively cause gene expression**. The existence of a particular gene within our DNA is not a predetermination or guarantee that our bodies will inherit a specific outcome. Your lifestyle, your mindset and beliefs form catalysts to start gene expression or obstructions to prevent a genetic trait from affecting health. Telling ourselves that we are immune from a particular disease is a starting point and the reverse is equally true. Beliefs are changeable, and gene suppression is possible. Genes are more like a gun containing bullets—loaded with potential, but the mind must pull the trigger.

This revelation is not merely scientific, but it is profoundly empowering. It reinforces what structured thought teaches: that our reality begins within, not outside. Through Lipton's insights, I came to see **belief itself as a potential biological tool**—capable of healing or harming, constructing or destroying.

- This understanding supports the **placebo and nocebo effects.**
- The body's physical response is a **biological mirror of beliefs**.
- Negative thought patterns create stress and disease.
- Positive thoughts foster healing and vitality.

Dr. Lipton's teachings resonate deeply with my own exploration into vibration, frequency, and conscious design. If thoughts are quantum vibrations and beliefs generate quantum energy, then we can understand the biological mechanism through which these vibrations become tissues, organs and flesh. The key message—that **you are not a victim of your genes but the mental-master of your biological systems**—echoes the call to personal mastery advocated in this book.

I often return to Lipton's central claim: "The moment you change your perception is the moment you rewrite the chemistry of your body." That sentence alone might contain the blueprint for transformation, and it is why *The Biology of Belief* sits among the foundational texts that inspired my work-in-progress toward a ***theory of everything***.

Quantum Thought?

Lipton's core thesis disrupts the long-dominant narrative of genetic determinism. He writes that genes are not fixed blueprints, but as responsive elements activated or silenced by signals from their environment. What is radical—and empowering—about this claim is Lipton's demonstration that the most significant of these signals are not external stimuli, but our internal beliefs. His research confirms that **the human mind does not merely interpret reality; it constructs the physiological response to it.**

This insight aligns with my thesis about consciousness as a quantum energy source, advanced throughout this book. If quantum energy is the intentional organization of mental processes to create coherent and positive life outcomes, Lipton provides the biological infrastructure that allows this architecture to manifest in physical form. Through the mechanism of epigenetic expression, **belief becomes biology.**

The Path of the New Human

---

*"I am seeking truth that extends
beyond knowledge."— Elmo*

The new human is not merely biologically advanced but spiritually and energetically awakened. The journey to becoming supernatural is the process of aligning inner frequencies with the highest expressions of one's purpose. It is a commitment to living in coherence, awareness, and creativity.

In the coming era, those who master the harmonics of thought and quantum mindfulness will lead to the evolution of civilization—not by force, but by resonance. They will anchor

124

peace, truth, and possibility through the vibration of their being.

Dr. Lipton's work harmonizes beautifully with the vibrational model proposed herein. Just as ancient frequencies like 432 Hz resonate through physical matter and consciousness, Lipton suggests that beliefs—carried as electrical impulses through the nervous system—can be considered frequencies themselves, instructing the cellular machinery on how to behave.

This reframing invites a synthesis of disciplines: neuroscience, quantum biology, psychology, and metaphysics. Belief, once viewed as an ephemeral construct, becomes a tangible agent of change. The placebo effect is no longer a curiosity; it is proof. The body heals when the mind believes in healing. Likewise, **the nocebo effect—where negative belief creates dysfunction**—proves the destructive potential of unchecked thought.

Integrating Lipton's findings into this chapter is not just an academic exercise. It is a call to action. It reinforces our power and responsibility to master structured thought, not only for mental clarity or emotional balance but for physical transformation and spiritual evolution. The union of Lipton's biology with our model of thought frequency may well be the keystone that bridges science and spirit.

As this book continues to explore the tools of entrainment, vibrational healing, and cognitive restructuring, let Dr. Lipton's work serve as both foundation and proof: **belief is not only powerful—it is biological.**

Take time to pause and reflect upon the future. We are threading many seemingly unrelated areas of knowledge into a new fabric to prepare ourselves for improvement in our minds and bodies. Now, you should be reaching an understanding, or a curiosity about **how to think like a polymath**, an essential quality as the world is spinning more rapidly and we must change ourselves to embrace these changes. The old familiar paths that were available to us yesterday are going to be repaved, as such we must learn how to navigate over new terrains. That is what learning is all about.

Learning Forever-more

To broaden our beliefs and capabilities, it is beneficial to adopt the approach of a **polymath, an individual whose curiosity and knowledge cover various and unrelated subjects.** By using AI, we can access extensive bodies of knowledge, enhancing personal growth, creativity, and critical thinking skills.

AI enables us to get diverse knowledge without extensive training or study. Learning should not be confined to a single subject area, particularly in the age of artificial intelligence, which does not require us to be specialists with a narrow focus. As the industrial and information era concludes, it is essential to adapt our education to embrace lifelong learning and expand our comfort zone to accommodate change. Our future survival depends on discovering new paths of awareness, adaptability, and collective consciousness.

Do you find the idea of being a polymath inspiring?

As we have become more aware of the subconscious blueprints that shape our experience, and the fact that thought influence matter at the quantum level, we gain the power to function as conscious designers of our own destiny. This leads us naturally to quantum mindfulness—a practice that aligns attention, intention, and emotion with quantum principles—action-at-a-distance (superposition). The following chapter bridges science and spirituality to offer practical tools for becoming a new kind of human—that is aware, intentional, and resonant with the deeper currents of reality. **Energetic currents run through the universe which is the source field of all consciousness.**

Conclusion

Supernatural possibilities for the internal transformation of the individual have been examined, and now attention is turned outward to collective consciousness. The evolution of self naturally influences the evolution of communities, institutions, and civilizations.

This next chapter will consider how shared awareness, values, and practices have gradually shaped our past and continually redefine humanity's collective future. The objective of becoming supernatural is to engage with spirit in a scientific manner. By channeling more power through each of us, we can consciously guide that evolution toward greater harmony, coherence, and love throughout the world.

Chapter 7: The Theology of Sovereignty

Introduction—Patterns of Awareness

"Ask, and it shall be given you; seek, and ye shall find; knock, and it shall be opened unto you: For every one that asketh receiveth; and he that seeketh findeth; and to him that knocketh it shall be opened."
Matthew 7:7–8 (KJV)

This verse is part of **Jesus' Sermon on the Mount** and it supposedly emphasizes the power of prayer, persistence, and faith. The phrase has since entered common usage, often detached from its true spiritual context, but its origin is unmistakably King James' version of biblical ideology.

Interestingly, a similar sentiment appears in **John 16:24**, where Jesus says:

"Ask, and ye shall receive, that your joy may be full."
John 16:24

Both verses reflect a theme of divine responsiveness, though always taught within the framework of God's will in accordance with his timing. Theologians have taught us this message in keeping with the vision of their king.

For centuries, the phrase *"Ask, and it shall be given you"* echoed from pulpits and scrolls, its promise cloaked in divine mystery. To the devout, it was a call to prayer. To the powerful, it may have been something far more literal—a coded truth about the nature of reality itself. In the age of quantum physics, where observation appears to influence the behavior of particles, the ancient words take on new resonance. Could it be that consciousness, long dismissed as passive, is in fact the architect of material existence?

The Quantum Veil

However, consider that this idea has evolved in modern interpretations of quantum physics. We could rethink of this bible passage, as taken from its theological traditions into a literal fact, as that is exactly what the latest scientific findings revealed. Our consciousness interacts with the physical realm giving way to changing and influencing the material world from the power rooted within us.

The following narrative has satisfied my curiosities as it weaves together biblical interpretation, quantum theory, historical power structures, and the idea of sovereign consciousness. It's a call to awaken from the pacifiers were placed over our mouths and our thoughts. We found this comforting in childhood, but we are no longer children, and I still had questions never answered by authorities. Those bible stories are still being preached in pulpits to the meek who would only inherit the earth in the afterlife.

This book aims to uncover the scientific means through which you are invited can redesign your blueprints. The hidden frequencies within the mind must be switched on, allowing our power to be transferred into physical reality. But we must engage a new set of empowering beliefs, taken with introspection and a newfound curiosity to discover the power of our birthright.

Modern quantum theory suggests that particles exist in a state of probability until observed. The act of observation collapses the wave function, bringing forth a tangible reality. This phenomenon—known as the observer effect—has led some physicists and philosophers to speculate that consciousness is not merely a witness to reality, but a participant in its creation. If this is true, then the biblical directive to "ask" may be more than spiritual metaphor. It may be a blueprint for manifestation.

Now consider the implications if such knowledge had been understood by ancient elites. Kings, popes, and noblemen—custodians of sacred texts and initiates of esoteric orders—may have interpreted these verses not as moral guidance, but as operational instructions. The masses were taught to pray for salvation, while the elite practiced intention as a tool of creation and took power away from others. The divide between doctrine and application became a mechanism of control.

Secret Societies

Secret societies throughout history—whether the Rosicrucian, Freemasons, or the inner circles of ecclesiastical power of Roman Catholicism—often guarded knowledge deemed too potent for public consumption. Theological truths that hinted at personal sovereignty were veiled in allegory or buried beneath ritual.

The divine spark within each of us *individually* has been obscured by layers of doctrine, religious, scientific and political hierarchy that's has encapsulated us in fear. To reveal that every person held the power to shape reality through focused thought and belief would have destabilized the very structures upon which empires were built, and sustained to this day.

Tithes and taxes—both extracted under the guise of duty, have functioned as parallel systems of energetic exchange, and are cleverly designed, as forms of enslavement at worst or servitude at its finest. One fed the church coffers, the other the state's revenues. Both relied on the belief that authority resided outside the self.

But what if the true temple is consciousness itself? What if the altar is intention, and the offering is attention? What if free will means an ability to satisfy both our

130

needs and to derive happiness as we live and thrive with every breath of freedom.

In this light, religious doctrine becomes less about salvation and more about suppression. The power structure depends on individuals believing they are incomplete, sinful, unworthy or powerless without external validation. Churches became the authorities that offered places of worship where you could be told what to believe, and to confess your misdeeds or face eternal damnation. Yet quantum insights suggest the opposite: that reality responds to belief regardless of religious doctrine, creed or dogmas, and that the universe may be participatory, not punitive.

To reclaim this truth is to step into sovereignty—not as rebellion, but as remembrance. Human souls inherited supernatural power as these are birth rights. The sovereign citizen is not merely a political construct, but a metaphysical one. It is the individual who recognizes that divinity is not some distant heavenly place, unreachable in everyday experiences, i.e., high above our material existence, but a state of being embedded within the soul.

Asking is not kneeling and begging, it is aligning and tuning our minds into that higher frequency, where heavenly awareness resonates to reshape our reality. The kingdom of heaven is not a place on higher ground, but a state of being consciously aware and consciously attuned to its frequency. We are creators forging our conceptual ideas into monuments as solid as granite.

This perspective represents an affirmation of individual sovereignty without any acts of defiance, but as the acknowledgement of our inherent rights. Individuals possess unique capabilities that may be viewed as fundamental aspects of their existence. Sovereignty is not solely a political concept but also encompasses one's recognition of internal potential. Divinity may be understood as an intrinsic quality, rather than something external or remote, and fulfillment is achieved through intentional alignment, rather than through supplication.

Theology, when stripped of its institutional armor, reveals a profound simplicity: that we are creators, not captives. That the sacred texts may have always pointed inward, not upward. And that the veil between science and spirit is thinner than we were led to believe.

In the end, the greatest heresy may be the belief that power lies elsewhere—above and beyond us. For those who dare to ask—not with fear, but with clarity—the answer may not come from the heavens above, but from within each of us. Courage is something deeply personal that begins in the deepest layers of our soul. Everyone has already been chosen, otherwise we could not have been born, as humans.

We are faced with limitless choices:
1. To exercise our free will with clarity, and walk boldly into a future where power comes with equal responsibility, or
2. To remain powerless and beholden unto others, or
3. To be held captive in fear; hiding from the unlimited power that was always within us, or
4. To choose leaders that we want follow, delegating our power and resources in service to their aims.

True power comes with immense responsibility. This knowledge is too powerful, and that is the King's rationale, the justification of why you were not taught these truths. Vast populations of peoples have been killed to satisfy an insatiable thirst for power and control. Acceptant of their unlimited authority was exchanged for lives.

Perhaps, those few that truly understood this did not trust others to rise ahead of them. Was this due to a lack of faith within themselves? Or did they fear that everyone might not act with kindness toward them? More unanswerable questions result from each intelligent question.

The response to openly telling others about this kind of knowledge became grounds for crucifixion, and thus secrecy promoted ignorance. And now comes artificial intelligence that will open new pathways for understanding and proving what was never understood or thought possible.

We must recognize this is why others who trembled when thinking about you being completed without their consent, dogma or baseless ideologies. They also feared how this powerful freedom would unravel the comfortable garments woven to carefully shield us from the raw and absolute truth.

Being created in the image of God, literally means you are a God. This was not meant as an analogy or a metaphor, as I was taught by church elders. Fear has been used to hold us back from what they are covertly seeking for themselves alone. Fear and ignorance immobilize us, it is mightier than the sword, and the enemy guarding knowledge keeps us distracted from the attainment of personal sovereignty.

Truth is immortal and therefore unchanged by deceptions or falsehoods. However, some longstanding beliefs must be reconsidered under the scrutiny of new evidence. The death of ignorance is observable as truth emerges into the clarity of daylight. For centuries the dark shadow of secrecy prevailed and now the time for concealment has ended.

Reclaiming Our Vital Force

We have entered yet another gilded age of enlightenment, where personal sovereignty is within our grasp, yet becoming supernaturally empowered will not come easily to all who hear of these facts. The human body is our temple and for many it lies in ruin from the self-inflicted damages affecting both mental and physical health.

The good news is that the loss of vitality caused by personal choices can usually be reversed, and the temple must be restored to full vitality. The fire that sustains our life force must be rekindled to reach our highest state of supernatural being. The steps required to repair, restore balance and vitality in the body can and must be addressed.

Part two of this book series goes deep into the strategic missions necessary to heal the body, making the light shine from within the temple. An in-depth exploration of evidence-based strategies for healing, supporting overall well-being and resilience lies ahead.

Awareness of these possibilities is the key to opening a doorway within the mind, but you must find courage and decide how to proceed with this vision. If it were easy, it would not have been so easily veiled, even by those who guarded this precious secret.

Suddenly a Genie Appears

You have read my mind, and that may be expanded into a metaphor: rubbing the magic bottle, and now the genie is looking through his crystal ball, asking, "what do you truly desire?" You have a spiritual soul that knows the right answer for you. For me, the answer would be to surrender all your powers to me, and I want that crystal ball.

But, setting aside my selfish humor, now you are filled with **Spiritual Sovereignty,** you have options and the potential for unlimited freedoms. There are many people that will continue their entire lives in relative obscurity accomplishing survival needs and a few pleasures. It will never come as a mandate that you ascend above the core instinctual behaviors that humans share alongside every animal on the tree of life.

This concept can be likened to seeking insight or guidance regarding one's true desires. Each individual possesses an intuition that can help determine the most appropriate course of action. While I may joke about wishing for absolute control or complete knowledge, it is important to return our focus on the broader perspective.

With expanded possibilities come greater choices and opportunities for autonomy. Most individuals will spend their lives fulfilling basic needs and enjoying occasional pleasures, remaining largely unnoticed. However, there is no inherent requirement to transcend the fundamental instincts shared by all animals; personal growth remains a voluntary pursuit.

Your desires and appetites will always be rationale choices, as it is your life alone to design. If you prefer enjoying short-term pleasures, prioritized before long-term sacrifices, no one will stop you. However, the consequences will arise—eventually! This is more than asking about your preferences in a hypothetical scenario. This is real life and even the smallest of your choices do matter. Life is not a rehearsal, we each have one life, one chance to live it to the fullest. Individuals have their own perspectives on what choices are best for them.

Everyone will be presented with multiple challenges, options and the possibility of increased involvement in society. Many individuals live their lives without significant contributions or public recognition, focusing on daily needs and some personal enjoyment. There is no requirement for people to act beyond basic instinctual behaviors common to humans and animals.

Personal desires and preferences may lead to prioritizing short-term enjoyment over long-term planning or any meaningful legacy. Observing animals, it is possible to see practical patterns in their behavior that could serve as useful examples. Adapting beneficial qualities found in nature could support personal development beyond mere survival. Although for many, fulfilling fundamental needs remains sufficient and seeking to make a difference that has lasting impacts upon our communities is too much to ask of them.

Others will reach their full potential by supporting humanitarian missions, addressing unmet needs with creative solutions, and their impactful contributions will be remembered as part of their enduring legacy.

Collective Evolution

As individuals awaken to the power of conscious creation, a natural extension unfolds shaping the collective future through shared insight. While individual awareness transforms personal destiny, patterns of awareness reveal how groups evolve through common beliefs, values, and intentions.

"Never doubt that a small group of thoughtful, committed citizens can change the world. Indeed, it is the only thing that ever has." — Margaret Mead

---

Cultural Evolution Through Conscious Design

Societies reflect the cumulative energy of their members. When enough individuals live in alignment with coherent principles, empathy, justice, sustainability—the society itself begins to shift. This is not merely philosophical. It is observable in movements that elevate civil rights, ecological awareness, and ethical technology.

Just as we reprogram our internal blueprint, we can reprogram the world around us. By designing systems rooted in integrity and well-being, we architect futures that serve generations to come. This is the essence of becoming supernatural as a species: moving beyond survival into stewardship. Machine intelligence will be aiding humans in unforeseen ways that will eliminate or alter all our survival needs.

Spiritual Technology and Inner Sovereignty

Spiritual technology refers to the methods by which we refine and realign our inner world. Practices such as meditation, sound healing, neurofeedback, yoga, and breathwork are not peripheral curiosities but vital tools of transformation. They allow us to navigate the noise of modern life, recover clarity, and establish coherence between body, mind, and soul. These tools are technologies in the truest sense—repeatable, measurable, and adaptable to different individuals—yet they operate on frequencies of consciousness that stimulate our internal biology, rather than mechanical hardware or drugs.

The promise of spiritual technology is not escapism but empowerment. By practicing regularly, we learn that sovereignty is not a matter of control over others but mastery of self. When enough individuals cultivate inner coherence, society itself shifts—education becomes more holistic, governance more ethical, communities more compassionate. We become less reactive to fear and more responsive to wisdom.

This journey often begins with a wakeup call, often accompanied by physical pain or mental stress. Many of us drift into unhealthy habits, unaware until the consequences arrive. *But first, the recognition—how did I get here? Then we must ask, how can I resolve my discomfort? And then, awareness becomes the threshold of transformation.*

Through determination and daily practice, we can reverse decline and rebuild vitality. Sovereignty is reclaimed not in isolation, but in renewed connection to intuition, purpose, and the greater flow of life.

Fictional Story: Metamorphosis

Once upon a time, in a secluded forest, there lived a wise teacher named Elora, whose wisdom was deeply rooted in nature's teachings. Elora's sanctuary was vibrantly adorned with flowers and butterflies that gracefully danced through sunlit air, embodying the results of transformation.

One day, a troubled young woman named Aria arrived at Elora's doorstep, burdened by years of dependence on substances that clouded her mind and weakened her spirit. Feeling trapped within her destructive habits, she yearned for liberation and a fresh start. My heart guided me to find something that I am not, and you are said to be in possession of great transformational knowledge.

Aria came to Elora seeking freedom from self-destructive habits and hoping for a new beginning. She believed Elora had supernatural powers that could help her change.

Elora welcomed Aria gently, guiding her to observe the caterpillars thriving in the garden. "Watch closely," she said, "And witness how your journey is reflected in nature."

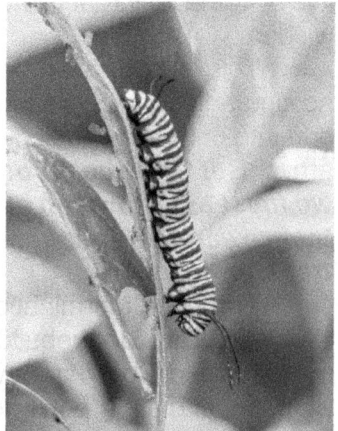

In the following weeks, Aria witnessed the remarkable process of metamorphosis. She watched how the caterpillar diligently spun its cocoon, surrendering into the silence of where transformation begins. Elora explained, "Change begins when we recognize that we can stop our old habits. You are like the caterpillar, and when that no longer serves your greater purpose, personal change, just like metamorphosis is possible."

Aria slowly learned to confront her habits, facing discomfort and challenges with courage and patience. Elora introduced her to natural remedies like soothing herbal teas and mindful meditation, helping Aria to gradually experience more inner peace and clarity.

Days turned to weeks, and Aria felt herself slowly transforming from within. Just as the caterpillar dissolved its former self in the cocoon, Aria shed the layers of her past dependencies, emerging stronger, wiser, and more vibrant.

Finally, the day arrived when Aria witnessed the butterfly breaking free from its cocoon, stretching its delicate wings for the very first time. Elora smiled warmly, saying,

"This is your true nature, Aria—a beauty and strength that has always existed within you. You are breaking free from your cocoon of old habits; you've finally allowed your inner self to emerge fully."

Aria, now replenished with a new self-confidence and feeling empowered, thanked Elora profoundly. Saying, "I am ready to embrace life with newfound vitality and purpose." *As she left the sanctuary, Elora reminded her, "Remember, Mother Nature teaches us how to meet Father Time gracefully. Embrace your transformation, for it is your path to happiness and your journey toward becoming supernatural."*

The Supernatural Journey

This book began as a vision—one seeded in the soul of a curious student seeking truth through science, spirit, religion and self-exploration. The journey led through the corridors of biology, chemistry, mathematics, electronics, and ultimately meditation. My journey had arrived at a design where consciousness became the living framework by which we evolve. *Our vulnerabilities and fears in childhood shape subconscious habits as we cope with situations in childish ways, as our brains aren't fully matured until around age 25.* As our brains mature, we gain the ability to consider consequences and intentionally change ourselves.

To become supernatural is not to transcend humanity, but to realize its highest form. It is to embrace creativity, compassion, and clarity as our natural state. It is to lead with vision, act with wisdom, and live with resonance. Human metamorphosis involves a change of heart and mind redirecting our conscious awareness.

The future awaits our design. Let us become the authors of a conscious civilization. Let us become supernatural in the age of AI. The integration of AI with human development requires an understanding of how thought and emotion influence behavior. It is important that our use of AI technologies reflect values aligned with human well-being. This means not just technical skills, but also moral insight. Technology should serve humanity, and artificial intelligence should support the pursuit of knowledge for the benefit of humankind. Utilizing all available written human knowledge has already provided AI with an estimation of what it means to be human, including our desires for emotional compassion and intellectual curiosity. We should expect that AI should inherit those intelligible facts as a part of its mission to aid us on our journey—as a complement to the mutual needs of all earthlings.

AI can support human emotional health through personalized mindfulness training or adaptive learning platforms tailored to individual talents and learning styles— thereby transforming education. AI could help human creativity by suggesting new harmonic patterns to a musician, a composer or visual ideas to an artist. For this to succeed, it is necessary to teach machines to recognize, rather than replicate, the deeper human motivations for meaning, truth, and connection.

Instincts from a Bygone Era

Fear is uniquely a biological instinct in natural living things, yet it will be perplexing to an artificial intelligence lacking the *"molecules of emotion"* that influence human and animal survival. We have explored how our mental states are aroused and how that affects the body.

Now, humans have introduced machine intelligence that will aid us on our journey towards becoming supernatural beings—completely freeing us from natural laws of the animal kingdom, means **survival of the fittest becomes a bygone era**. Survival instincts from our evolutionary past triggered our actions--eventually fading away--becoming less likely to affect our future behaviors as we are becoming supernatural beings.

Conclusion

Before we can reach our destination, we must return to the body—our most immediate instrument of transformation. The mind connects us with the physical realm through our brain—which resides in the physical realm—our physiology. Consciousness must be embodied to manifest fully in the world.

This chapter and earlier ones outlined frameworks for mental evolution and introduced theoretical concepts important for mindfulness and intentionality. Health and self-care are presented as essential aspects of well-being, particularly given risks beyond individual control. The next chapter moves beyond ideological discussion to practical considerations, exploring the ongoing process of personal and planetary change, while acknowledging existing challenges.

Chapter 8: Beyond Theoretical Foundations

Introduction

Looking ahead, it has become clear that the initial scope of my vision was overly broad; too much for a single book. Yet, my approach to addressing the various factors influencing overall health and wellbeing had to be grounded in principles supported by ancient systems. Recent advancements demonstrate that artificial intelligence is successfully interpreting historic manuscripts, uncovering fresh perspectives through quantum computational power. Our most advanced machine intelligence continues to drive breakthroughs across numerous domains, offering promising developments for society.

However, studies on negativity bias confirm our inclination to focus more intensely on negative experiences—an evolutionary trait rooted deeply in human psychology, allowing ancient humans to recognize and avoid threats quickly.

Neuroscientist John T. Cacioppo demonstrated that our brains exhibit stronger neural processing when confronted with negative stimuli compared to positive ones. Thus, incentives matter greatly. If humans respond instinctively to fear, anxiety, and threats, industries built upon sensationalism will continue to thrive unless consciously disrupted. So, our next steps along this journey will be to address issues effectively through negative motivation.

Humans think and then respond in strange ways, so we must do what works, rather than what seems logical.

First Comes Bad News

Bad news travels swiftly; good news seems mundane by comparison. Media outlets understand human nature's inherent attraction to negative information.

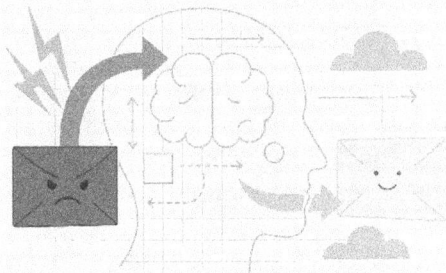

After extensive work on this manuscript, I have recognized that the hypothesis—achieving a 'supernatural' state in the age of AI—is increasingly attainable for many individuals. However, this consideration naturally leads to an examination of human nature, particularly in relation to habit formation and the establishment of enduring beliefs. So, we must investigate what's going on in the psychology of normal human activities, motives, and routines. Any deviations from normal comes through new motives.

The foundational principle in economics, that "people respond to incentives," reflects one of the core aspects of human behavior. Consequently, it is necessary to refine my approach in addressing both positive and negative information to more accurately reflect the underlying incentive structures at play. People seem to be moved into action when they know severe consequences likely to occur or have already arrived. Then they act, as if they would in *reaction.*

My objective is to inspire, inform, and motivate individuals to realize their highest potential within the scope of their personal agency. Observation reveals that people will fiercely defend even their known shortcomings, before any possibility for change can emerge. Fear motivates us to move faster than rationales or logic. The church and our governments have succeeded in this proven concept.

143

Accordingly, I am addressing the challenges and concerns about external influences upfront, allowing us to systematically overcome obstacles and move beyond apprehension towards growth and achievement.

Illuminating Through Consciousness

True transformation, therefore, requires intentionality—pouring sunlight over the shadows of unconscious habitual behavior. Neuroscience shows us clearly that neuroplasticity allows brains to reshape thought patterns, even deeply ingrained ones.

Neuroplasticity means our brains have evolved to be flexible, to learn, to adapt and to rethink, rewire internal circuitry. This enables new beliefs, ideas or adaptability to both internal and external changes in the environment. The brain is reprogrammable and therein lies our greatest advantage as human beings. We can change our minds, both literally and figuratively.

Researchers like Dr. Joe Dispenza demonstrate through extensive studies how focused meditation and mindfulness practices can structurally alter the brain, empowering individuals to reshape their responses to external stimuli and break free from reactive cycles. I gleaned this understanding through 10 years of firsthand practice using biofeedback for meditation and how it dramatically enhanced my cognitive experience.

Meditation opens the gateway to reducing stress hormones leading to a calmer, more steady state of being. Part Two in this book series takes a deep dive into this practice.

We must realize our power and agency as individuals. Collective consciousness reflects the sum of individual wills, as such, personal transformation will bear its fulfillment in societal implications. Our individual willpower can be greater or less impactful relative to others, but the whole of humanity causes our mutual experience.

Princeton's Global Consciousness Project conducted experiments that suggest our shared human consciousness measurably responds to and impacts global events, thus reinforcing the idea that individual contributions can significantly shape or steer collective experiences.

Navigating Environmental Realities

The interplay between environment and health is undeniable. Historical evidence of industrial pollution—such as the catastrophic Minamata Bay mercury poisoning in Japan or the Flint water crisis in Michigan—illustrates corporations prioritizing profit over human well-being until forcibly regulated.

Monsanto's engineering of sterile corn seeds and widespread sales for the application of carcinogenic chemicals like glyphosate (Roundup) underscore the perils of unregulated profit motives. Scientific literature confirms glyphosate's toxicity, with landmark lawsuits affirming its carcinogenicity despite decades of corporate denial.

Furthermore, Agent Orange, initially deployed as a tool for chemical warfare, was transitioned to consumer agricultural products, showing a troubling continuity in the normalization of harmful chemical practices.

Government and corporate accountability remain limited and historical precedents—such as the extensive Agent Orange litigation—underscore the necessity for vigilant public oversight.

But first comes a reiteration of what has already been well discussed, yet it comes into focus in the context of my warnings about health consequences introduced by environmental risks, beyond our immediate awareness or control.

Flint Water Crisis

As a lifelong resident in the State of Michigan, I anticipate that some of my readers are in close proximity to

145

our local news about the Flint water crisis. General Motors played a central role in this contamination. Throughout much of the 20th century, GM's factories in Flint released significant amounts of industrial waste, including heavy metals, oils, and solvents directly into the river. Although environmental regulations gradually improved with the advent of the Clean Water Act in 1972, damage from earlier decades had already altered the river's ecosystem and its water quality became toxic.

When the City of Flint switched its water supply to the Flint River in April 2014 without adequate corrosion control, the river's corrosive nature leached lead from aging pipes, compounding the problem and resulting in a public health disaster. Water that could be corrosive to pipes was surely unthinkable for human consumption.

In addition to GM, other industries operating in and around Flint contributed to the degradation of the river. Wastewater from landfills, agriculture, and runoff from storm drains also played roles. However, GM remains the most prominently cited contributor due to its historical scale and impact on the local environment.

The Flint crisis underscores the intersection of environmental neglect, industrial legacy, and governance or policy failure. The suggestion that we need to bring manufacturing back into the United States makes me cringe. It could be another foolish notion. Industrial pollutions from the previous century have not been fully remediated.

You might ponder to think, he may be hinting at blind faith paired with elite detachment, and that would be correct.

People get motivated by rhetorical nonsense and then forget about the bigger picture, the existing context and consequences of manufacturing in the not-too-distant past. Jobs are desirable, yet pollution from industrial waste is still killing us. I cannot forget the documentary coming into my YouTube feed about pollution in Beijing China. Make America Polluted Again!

146

Proactive Corporate Regulation

Legislators today are increasingly influenced, even manipulated—by corporate lobbyists who argue that environmental and safety regulations are harming the economy by driving up the cost of manufacturing in America. But let us be clear: the cost of doing the right thing from the start would have been far less than the cost of repairing the damage caused by corporate negligence.

Regulations exist because history has repeatedly shown that without oversight, profits often come at the expense of public health, worker safety, and the natural world. The consequences of corporate overreach nearly always arrive after the damage has already been done. This is why regulations are not just bureaucratic red tape; they are necessary safeguards grounded in rational foresight.

We must ask ourselves: which costs truly matter? Is the bottom line of a quarterly report more valuable than clean air, drinkable water, and the long-term health of our communities? Prioritizing manufacturing profits over environmental protection and public health is a dangerous trade-off. The real cost is not found on a balance sheet—it is measured in ecosystems destroyed, lives shortened, and trust eroded.

Only regulations that carry meaningful, enforceable consequences, including criminal penalties where appropriate—can deter those who might sacrifice the greater good for financial gain. These measures are not anti-business; they are pro-responsibility. They protect both people and the planet from unchecked greed, and they ensure that progress does not come at an irreparable price.

Argument supporting unregulated corporate trust, where profit comes before the environment is irrational at best, deadly at its worst. We have seen how corporate decision making worked in the past. What incentive do corporations have other than profits?

Now, comes more bad news, as we listen to political talking points and forget about the existing facts and consequences at ground zero of the automotive industrial revolution in Michigan. The Flint water crisis is one of the many consequences of the industrial era.

Another Auto Recall

Maybe your memory should be automatically recalled, remembering context of the nightmares brought upon the public by manufacturing. American corporate boardrooms originally found the land of the free was profitable, until the EPA was created to protect American citizens from corporate crimes against our society.

In the late 20th century, U.S. auto manufacturers began relocating production overseas to remain competitive in a rapidly globalizing economy. That was a good excuse sold to us, as consumers. The hidden agenda and the driving force was *cost efficiency—**foreign labor markets offered significantly lower wages, fewer regulatory constraints, and often looser environmental standards***.

Corporations saw an opportunity to cut expenses by tapping into these conditions, maximizing profits while keeping vehicle prices the same or even higher. Every vehicle that I have ever purchased came with increasingly higher prices regardless of offshoring.

As trade agreements opened new doors, the offshoring trend accelerated, decimating industrial hubs like Detroit. The shift wasn't just economic, it exposed a deeper ethical dilemma: the pursuit of profit at the expense of vulnerable labor populations and the environment, both abroad and at home.

The shift towards international manufacturing was, in part, influenced by reduced scrutiny and less stringent environmental regulations abroad. These factors should be carefully considered when evaluating the future of domestic industry and its broader implications.

Current Status

As of 2025, significant progress has been made in replacing contaminated lead service lines. Criminal cases continue against state and city officials. Water quality has improved, but long-term trust in public institutions remains damaged.

Restoring Health After Exposure

People exposed to contaminated water—especially children—should follow a comprehensive approach to mitigate long-term effects:

1. Medical Testing and Monitoring:
   o Blood tests for levels of lead poisoning, particularly for children.
   o Ongoing developmental screenings and neuropsychological assessments.
2. Nutritional Support:
   o Diets high in calcium, iron, and vitamin C help reduce lead absorption and assist the body in excreting lead.
   o Promote foods such as leafy greens, beans, citrus fruits, and eggs, and whole grains.
3. Educational Support:
   o Early childhood education and intervention services for developmental delays.
   o School-based health programs for cognitive and behavioral monitoring.
4. Detoxification and Holistic Therapies:
   o **Safe Chelation Therapy is under medical supervision in severe cases.** I have documented this treatment protocol for in-depth study in Part Two of this book.
   o Encourage hydration with clean, filtered water.
   o Consider therapies like sauna, antioxidant support (vitamin E, selenium, glutathione), and functional medicine to aid cellular recovery.

5. Mental Health Services:
   - Counseling for trauma, stress, and trust-related issues stemming from institutional failure.
6. Community and Policy Action:
   - Ongoing advocacy for clean water access, transparency, and government accountability.
   - Participation in public health monitoring initiatives and environmental justice movements.

The Flint Water Crisis is not only a cautionary tale about infrastructure and environmental negligence but also a call for systemic reform and community empowerment.

Restoring health requires more than emergency medical treatment, it demands a holistic, sustained response rooted in justice, education, and resilience. Governmental agencies and the medical establishment are insufficient, we must protect ourselves and restore our health through self-care.

Self-Care as Essential Medicine

Given these environmental challenges, proactive self-care emerges not merely as a luxury but as an urgent imperative. Your **thoughts form the front line of a health defense system**. The American Journal of Preventive Medicine highlights prevention as more effective than reactive medical treatment and this should not come as a surprise. We must join in emphasizing lifestyle modifications to reduce chronic disease risk.

Traditional and alternative medicine has validated numerous methods for detoxification of our bodies. Water fasting, herbal supplementation, chelation therapy, and dietary interventions are examples underscoring the powerful role of individual responsibility in self-care.

Part Two of this journey examines dozens of self-healing modalities that do not involve pharmaceutical drugs, and it provides a deep discussion of my personal experiences with these alternatives. Doctors rarely tell patients that a pharmaceutical will cure an illness. Yet, that expectation can shape everything from how patients adhere to treatments to how they emotionally respond to outcomes.

WHEN A DOCTOR SAYS, "TAKE THIS," THE IMPLICIT HOPE IS OFTEN, "THIS WILL FIX ME."

Even if doctors use more measured language, the emotional need for certainty often will fill in any gaps in the communication. It's human to want an immediate resolution in moments of personal vulnerability, especially, while suffering from pains during those delicate discussions.

We all want to feel better, and the "doctor knows best" was drummed into our heads during early childhood experiences. Those expectations persist into adulthood, and until ultimately death doeth us part from this indoctrination, a belief system.

Thus, the disconnects between medical treatments and patient expectations can lead to disappointments, or even mistrust, if recovery doesn't follow as anticipated.

Compassionate communication matters so deeply—not just conveying clinical facts but aligning those facts with the patient's emotional expectations and drawing a realistic picture of the individual's actual health landscape.

It's not enough to say what a drug does—we also must talk about what it might not do or what side effects might arise.

It is important to consider how broader trends, such as pharmaceutical marketing strategies, influence your expectations. Additionally, the public perception of so-called *miracle cures"* is often shaped by these external factors.

My aim is to avoid being the target of pharmaceutical advertising

Advertising plays a significant role in guiding consumer decision-making by highlighting what should be avoided or preferred. The intent behind such campaigns is to shape attitudes and behaviors in ways that would not necessarily align with one's natural inclinations without promotional influence.

Breaking the Chains of External Authority

The phrase "The Doctor Knows Best" was popularized by the 1960s British science fiction series *Doctor Who*.

The sentiment—trusting the Doctor's wisdom and authority—became a thematic cornerstone of the show. The Doctor, a time-traveling alien with vast knowledge and moral conviction, often made decisions that others questioned, only to be proven right in the end.

This cultivated a cultural shorthand for trusting medical or scientific expertise, especially when delivered while enshrouded in a white coat and delivered with expertise, confidence and charm.

That said, the phrase also echoes a broader societal trope from mid-20th-century media, where authority figures—especially doctors—were portrayed as infallible.

It's possible the phrase gained traction through a combination of television, advertising, and cultural norms of the era. Somehow, these sentiments came to us through the media to represent every level of authority.

Institutions,—governmental, corporate, educational, or medical—often prioritize systemic stability and profitability over individual welfare.

Social psychologist Stanley Milgram's obedience experiments starkly illustrate the human tendency to defer moral responsibility to perceived authority figures.

Yet, historical figures like Ralph Waldo Emerson and Henry David Thoreau advocated fiercely for individual sovereignty, autonomy, and self-governance as remedies for societal conformity and passive obedience. As a high school student, Emerson's essay, "Self-Reliance" set the stage, identifying my character traits.

Towards Personal and Collective Sovereignty

We must therefore reframe our conception of authority and truth. Cognitive psychology emphasizes how deeply childhood conditioning shapes adult beliefs. Yet research by Carol Dweck on growth mindset reveals our potential to continually update and refine our belief systems through conscious intention and sustained effort. Sovereignty, therefore, requires diligent internal cultivation of critical thinking, skepticism toward authority, and profound self-awareness.

Hypnosis and Awakening

Human behavior often resembles hypnosis, driven by subconscious conditioning rather than conscious choice. Hypnosis research by neuroscientist Amir Raz confirms how suggestible the human mind is—how easily external stimuli and authoritative suggestions shape perception and behavior. Thus, awakening from societal hypnosis means reclaiming self-awareness, actively reconstructing our inner narrative, and consciously defining our authentic identities.

It is important to recognize the potential of self-hypnosis as a method for influencing and reconstructing the internal frameworks within the subconscious mind that shape personal identity. Through neuroplasticity, individuals can enhance their capacity to operate autonomously—avoiding societal pressures, while still fulfilling their moral and ethical responsibilities to family, community, and society at large. Each person possesses inherent abilities that, over time, may contribute positively to the collective advancement of humanity.

Becoming Supernatural: A Practical Vision

Ultimately, the transformation described throughout this book series demands disciplined inner work and external vigilance. Cutting-edge research in cellular biology, neuroscience, and epigenetics validates the idea that humans are not victims or bystanders of circumstance but potent creators of personal reality. To believe otherwise is to dimmish your self-worth and deny your value as a human being.

Dr. Bruce Lipton's research on epigenetics confirms that environmental perceptions profoundly influence genetic expression, validating the concept that our thoughts and beliefs directly shape our biological experiences.

To truly become supernatural beings in the age of AI, we must commit to proactive, intentional mastery of consciousness. Aiming at the stars could create a shooting star, or at least a personal landing on the moon.

Harnessing insights found in ancient wisdom, neuroscience, quantum mechanics, and psychological research is our foundational strategy. Next, we call upon ourselves to develop core abilities to cultivate profound internal coherence, rooted in resolute internal alignment of intention.

Bridges to Practical Application

Thus, we are reaching closure of Part One, firmly grounded in theoretical underpinnings for a new science of mind, body and soul. Readers are now equipped to engage consciously, empowered by awareness of human psychology, environmental realities, institutional biases, and their own profound potential for this unique transformation into supernatural beings using AI as our agents for progress.

The following preview highlights many integrative and alternative health strategies to be introduced in **Part Two** of this series.

154

Six Systems—Health Modalities

1) Measurement & Insight
   Purpose: Establish baseline metrics and track progress over time.
   a. Heart Rate Variability (HRV)
   b. Blood Pressure Monitoring Devices
   c. EEG Biofeedback Devices
   d. Biometric Impedance
   e. Ketone Meters
   f. Journaling & Self-Assessment Tools

2) Light & Electromagnetic Therapies
   Purpose: Influence cellular function and circadian alignment.
   a. Photobiomodulation / Red Light Therapy
   b. Pulsed Electromagnetic Frequency (PEMF) Devices
   c. Sungazing (with safety guidelines)
   d. Royal Rife Frequency Devices *(with evidence discussion)*

3) Nervous System Regulation
   Purpose: Train autonomic balance and mental calm.
   a. Mindfulness Meditation
   b. Binaural Beats
   c. Brainwave Frequencies Training
   d. Biofeedback (general)
   e. Whole Body Vibration (WBV) for neuro-muscular, blood and lymph stimulation

4) Breath, Temperature & Energetic Practices
   Purpose: Enhance oxygenation, circulation, and resilience.
   a. Wim Hof Breathing Technique
   b. Infrared Sauna
   c. Earth Grounding
   d. Structured Water (as an energetic input)

5) Manual & Structural Therapies
   Purpose: Align and strengthen structural integrity.

155

a. Chiropractic
b. Rolfing
c. Deep Tissue Massage
d. Reflexology
e. Exercise

6) Nutrition & Botanical Approaches

Purpose: Support biochemistry through natural inputs.
a. Water
b. Food As Medicine
c. Fasting / OMAD Protocols
d. Juicing
e. Herbal Remedies
f. Essential Oils
g. Food Grade Hydrogen Peroxide *(with safety guidance)*
h. Chelation Therapy (under supervision)

Table 8.1

Table 8.1 - Comparison of Natural Health Practices

Modality	Primary Effects	Onset Time	Evidence Level	Time & Cost Factors
HRV Monitoring	Stress tracking, recovery readiness	Immediate feedback	Strong	1–2 min/day; low device cost
Mindfulness Meditation	Calm, focus, emotional regulation	Short to long term	Strong	10–20 min/day; free or low cost
Red Light Therapy	Pain relief, tissue repair	Short to mid-term	Moderate	5–20 min/day; device investment
Wim Hof Breathing	Energy, stress tolerance	Immediate to short term	Emerging	10–15 min/day; no cost
Chiropractic	Pain relief, mobility	Immediate to short term	Moderate	Weekly; provider fees
Fasting / OMAD	Weight control, metabolic reset	Days to weeks	Strong	Daily habit; no cost

Part Two serves as a comprehensive resource offering practical advice on optimizing physical health and its significance in enhancing mental processes that may support advanced cognitive abilities. It addresses the interconnectedness of mind, body, and spirit as integral elements, which collectively foster heightened awareness and influence subtle quantum energies.

It may come as a surprise to learn how your intentions cause the release of raw quantum energy transmitted through us as concentration of entrained thought gets empowered by emotions. Our brainwaves serve as broadcast transceivers perceiving, listening, causing, effecting and completing actions that change the mental and physical realm.

The mechanisms underlying consciousness—its design, purpose, and integration are broken apart—illuminating the foundational aspects for limitless human potential. The concept of the soul is presented as entering the physical realm via DNA, with the human body regarded as a temporary vessel facilitating creative development. Intentionality initiates emotional responses that fuel progress, and it is suggested that positive emotions such as love serve as powerful drivers of creative and transformative energy.

We now complete **Part One**, which has armed us with foundational knowledge, readying for the actionable wisdom awaiting us—an exploration into powerful, non-invasive health modalities that will guide us toward our ultimate goal as supernatural beings.

Next, we must focus upon repair and regeneration of our bodies to realize supernatural living. A powerful mind requires a healthy body to achieve its aims and the business of living a supernatural experience in the place and time where artificial intelligence provides us with access to ancient, contemporary and worldwide sources of wisdom.

Part Two provides practical guides for self-care utilizing natural health practices that can be beneficial to alleviate chronic illnesses. It is important to recognize that some health

158

modalities may depend on specific tools or professional guidance to meet your interests or needs.

Engaging in a variety of practices overlapping one another can increase the likelihood of positive outcomes. These practices can enhance overall well-being through self-healing activities, and some will require professional practitioners. No side effects are likely, because no prescription drugs are involved.

Part Three probes how the power plant within our brain acts as a storehouse of consciousness. How it is designed with mathematical symmetry, its purpose, and how each soul creates its unique human body using the blueprints written in our DNA.

The human body serves as an individualized experience for a greater whole to access. We must unveil the memory of our soul, and its foundation for supernatural existence in the physical realm. The pathway is illuminated, and it leads us directly to understand that our bodies are temporary housing: shelters for the soul serving as an access point to creative progress.

Grand Conclusion

As we conclude Part One, let us pause to gather the essential insights and prepare for the journey ahead. The ideas explored thus far provide a foundation, but they also point toward a practical path that you can begin walking today. What follows is a distillation of our key lessons, the obstacles that remain, the promise of what comes next, and a simple first step to carry forward into Part Two.

What we now know

We have uncovered that human potential is not singular but threefold—mind, body, and soul—woven together through universal patterns of harmonic resonance. Factor-9 mathematics, the laws of vibration, and the realities of energy all reveal that life's architecture is both ordered and expansive. We now know:

- Human capacity extends far beyond survival; it is patterned for creativity, transformation, and transcendence.
- The greatest barriers are rarely natural but are instead inherited stories, limiting beliefs and habits that shape our lives.
- Consciousness, when disciplined and focused, is not passive—it actively reshapes reality, as surely as technology reshapes the external world.

What blocks us

Despite this knowledge, certain sub-conscious and emotional forces continue to restrain us:

- Cultural systems—government, religion, media—often divert or dilute personal empowerment, channeling it into conformity rather than creativity.
- Within ourselves, personal inertia persists. The pull of distraction, the comfort of routine, and the fear of

change keep us from stepping fully into transformation.

What changes will come in Part Two

Part Two of this book series invites you to move from theory to practice. The focus shifts to the real, tangible modalities that can restore balance and vitality in everyday life. Ancient wisdom converges with modern science, offering tools that are both timeless and timely. In the chapters ahead you will explore:

- Nutrition that supports cellular repair and long-term health.
- Light and sound therapies that recalibrate body and mind.
- Breathwork and mindfulness practices awaken clarity and resilience.
- Part II is about walking the path, not merely knowing it. These are not abstract ideas but lived experiences.

Your next step today

Transformation begins with something small—an action you can take right now. Pause for a moment and take five deliberate, deep breaths. Notice how each inhale expands your chest, and each exhale releases tension. This single act is a seed of self-mastery: it awakens awareness, centers your body, and begins to align your inner state with the outer world.

Tomorrow, you must begin the **7-Day On Ramp**, a practical series of daily exercises that build momentum for the larger practices described in Part Two. Each day adds one step toward aligning thought, body, and spirit, preparing you for the deeper transformation that awaits.

We have laid the theoretical foundation in Part One:
1. Our states of consciousness are causal,
2. Coherence is a trainable state, and

3. The necessity of mastering thought–emotion–frequency alignment.

Knowledge alone cannot transform lives—it must be embodied through consistent, measurable practice. We stand at the threshold of application, where abstract principles become daily actions. The next step is to choose deliberate practices, tracking your results to build a personal operating protocol.

In Part Two, we move from theory to practical training, transforming insight into sustainable, repeatable habits that underpin abundant mental and physical wellness. You must achieve complete self-control to embrace your full potential and thereby begin living in a supernatural experience.

"Love is the supreme creative force"—
Elmo

Appendix A –Glossary of Key Terminology & Ideas

A

Artificial Intelligence (AI) – Computer software systems capable of performing tasks that normally require human intelligence, such as learning, reasoning, and perception; discussed as both a tool and a threat depending on personal goals or alignment. – pg. 3, 4, 12, 13, 15, 16, 18, 38, 64, 85, 97, 114, 116, 122, 135, 142-3, 145, 162

Awakening – The process of becoming consciously aware of deeper truths regarding self, society, and the universe; often a precursor to personal or spiritual transformation. – pg. 14, 20, 23, 55, 71, 156

B

Becoming Supernatural – The ability to transcend ordinary mental and physical limitations through practices that harmonize body, mind, and soul. – p 3, 14, 15, 16, 17, 18, 20, 21, 22, 23, 24, 52, 55, 66, 72, 73, 88, 95, 102, 115, 116, 118, 119

Biofield – The electromagnetic and subtle energy fields purported to surround and permeate the human body; considered integral to healing. – pg. 99

Biofeedback – A method of gaining awareness and control over physiological functions using electronic monitoring to influence mental and physical well-being. – pg. 148, 160

Body-Mind-Spirit – A triadic framework acknowledging the interdependence of physical health, psychological state, and spiritual awareness. – pg. 114, 121, 140

Brainwaves – Rhythmic patterns of neural activity in the brain; linked with various states of consciousness. – pg. 92, 93, 98, 99, 160, 163

C

Cacioppo, John T. – pg. 145

Coherence – A state in which heart, brain, and body systems operate in harmonious rhythm, producing optimal health and cognitive function. – pg. 5, 14, 16, 81, 89, 95, 99, 101, 102, 115, 116, 122, 128, 130, 140, 158, 167

Consciousness – The state of being aware of and able to think and perceive; considered causal and participatory in the architecture of reality. – pg. 3, 4, 13, 14, 17, 18, 20, 21, 22, 27, 61, 66, 67, 69, 70, 71, 76, 83, 88, 92, 97, 99, 104, 106, 116, 117, 119, 121, 123, 127, 128, 130, 132, 134, 140

D

Duality – The two-fold nature of reality; principle of opposing forces, where intent and unintended consequences are observable. – pg. 8, 37, 76, 111

E

EEG – Electroencephalography; a method for recording electrical activity of the brain, often used in meditation and neurofeedback practices. – pg. 160

Energy Medicine – Healing modalities based on the manipulation or influence of the body's subtle energies rather than chemical or surgical interventions. – See part two

F

Frequency – The rate at which a vibration occurs; in this context, associated with states of consciousness and biological resonance. – pg. 5, 21, 67, 78, 87, 89, 90, 91, 92, 93, 94, 95, 99, 128, 132, 134, 140, 160, 167

H

Heart-Brain Connection – The idea that the heart's electromagnetic field interacts with the brain, affecting emotion, cognition, and coherence. – pg. 14, 15, 16

Heart Disease – pg. 40, 41

Heart Rate Variability (HRV) – pg. 160

Harmonic Cosmology – The notion that mathematics serves as the unifying musical score for natural phenomena; the resonant harmony and order found in nature and within living systems. - pg. 74, 76, 77, 79, 81, 90, 91, 94, 99, 100, 101, 130

I

Iatrogenic Illness – Harm that occurs due to medical treatments, errors in diagnosis, prescription drugs that conflict with one another, known drug side effects, surgical mistakes, hospital-acquired infections, or adverse effects of therapeutic procedures. pg. 40, 41

Intuition – Introspection or perceptions that are independent of physical evidence, rational processes, often associated with insight and spiritual guidance. – pg. 47, 72, 99, 137

J

Jungian Psychology – A school of psychology founded by Carl Jung that emphasizes the collective unconscious, archetypes, and individuation. – See part two

K

Kundalini – A form of latent spiritual energy believed to reside at the base of the spine and rise through the chakras during awakening. – See part two

L

Lipton, PhD., Bruce – pg. 124-129, 158

M

Meditation – A disciplined practice used to focus the mind, alter consciousness, and promote spiritual growth and physiological healing. – pg. 98, 113, 148

Mind-Body-Soul Interface – The dynamic interaction between mental states and physical health, emphasizing psychosomatic relationships. – pg. 74

Morphogenic Fields – Hypothesized fields proposed by Rupert Sheldrake that shape the development of biological forms and behaviors. – See part 2

Mysticism – The pursuit of union with the divine or ultimate reality through inward practices and direct personal experience. – See part 2

N

Neurofeedback – A biofeedback technique using real-time EEG data to teach self-regulation of brain function. – pg. 140

Neuroplasticity – The brain's ability to reorganize itself by forming new neural connections in response to learning or injury. – pg. 15, 107, 115, 148

P

Pert, Dr., Candace – pg. 96-97

Photon Emission – The release of light particles from biological systems, sometimes interpreted as evidence of cellular communication or consciousness. – pg. 120

Pineal Gland – An endocrine gland in the brain often associated with spiritual insight, circadian rhythms, and the "third eye." – See part 2

Placebo Effect – A beneficial health outcome resulting from a person's belief in the efficacy of a treatment that has no therapeutic value. – pg. 126

Plato – pg. 76, 81, 82, 91

Prayer and Intention – The conscious focusing of thought and emotion to influence personal reality or collective outcomes. – pg. 131

Pythagoras – pg. 76, 90

V

Vibration – The oscillation of particles or energy fields; often discussed in relation to frequency, resonance, and healing. – pg. 15, 67, 74, 86, 87, 88, 89, 90, 91, 92, 95, 99, 126, 128, 160, 165

W

We Inside Me (Triune Self) – A framework for understanding the layered nature of self-awareness and personal identity across physical, emotional, and spiritual dimensions. – pg. 53, 70, 86, 103

Bibliography

Parts One, Two & Three

This bibliography lists authors whose works were referenced or written on topics discussed in this book series. It includes references for Parts One, Two, and Three. The bibliography provides an overview of the range and depth of sources used throughout the trilogy and may serve as a resource for further study.

Achor, Shawn. 2010. "The Happiness Advantage: The Seven Principles of Positive Psychology That Fuel Success and Performance at Work." New York: Crown Business.

Alexander, Eben. 2012. "Proof of Heaven: A Neurosurgeon's Journey into the Afterlife." New York: Simon & Schuster.

Amen, Daniel G. 2011. "Change Your Brain, Change Your Life: The Breakthrough Program for Conquering Anxiety, Depression, Obsessiveness, Lack of Focus, Anger, and Memory Problems." New York: Harmony.

Attia, Peter. 2023. "Outlive: The Science and Art of Longevity." New York: Harmony.

Barrett, Lisa Feldman. 2017. "How Emotions Are Made: The Secret Life of the Brain." New York: Houghton Mifflin Harcourt.

Becker, Robert O., and Gary Selden. 1985. "The Body Electric: Electromagnetism and the Foundation of Life." New York: William Morrow.

Bell, Fred. 1995. "Death of Ignorance." Pyradyne Publishing.

Bohm, David. 1980. "Wholeness and the Implicate Order." London: Routledge.

Braden, Gregg. 2000. "The Isaiah Effect: Decoding the Lost Science of Prayer and Prophecy." New York: Harmony.

Brown, Brené. 2012. "Daring Greatly: How the Courage to Be Vulnerable Transforms the Way We Live, Love, Parent, and Lead." New York: Gotham.

Campbell, T. Colin, and Thomas M. Campbell. 2006. "The China Study: The Most Comprehensive Study of Nutrition Ever Conducted." Dallas, TX: BenBella Books.

Carroll, Sean. 2016. "The Big Picture: On the Origins of Life, Meaning, and the Universe Itself." New York: Dutton.

Chambers, Becky. 2013. "Whole Body Vibration: The Future of Good Health." Vibrant Health.

Chevalier, Gaétan. 2012. "Reconnect to the Earth: The Benefits of Earthing." Kindle Edition.

Chopra, Deepak. 1993. "Ageless Body, Timeless Mind: The Quantum Alternative to Growing Old." New York: Harmony.

Church, Dawson. 2019. "Mind to Matter: The Astonishing Science of How Your Brain Creates Material Reality." Carlsbad, CA: Hay House.

Dispenza, Joe. 2017. "Becoming Supernatural: How Common People Are Doing the Uncommon." Carlsbad, CA: Hay House.

Dweck, Carol S. 2006. "Mindset: The New Psychology of Success." New York: Random House.

Emerson, Ralph Waldo. 1841. "Self-Reliance and Other Essays." Boston: James Munroe and Company.

Fredricks, Randi. 2012. "Fasting: An Exceptional Human Experience." Kindle Edition.

Gawdat, Mo. 2017. "Solve for Happy: Engineer Your Path to Joy." New York: Gallery Books.

Gerber, Richard. 2001. "Vibrational Medicine: The #1 Handbook of Subtle-Energy Therapies." Bear & Company.

Goleman, Daniel. 1995. "Emotional Intelligence: Why It Can Matter More Than IQ." New York: Bantam Books.

Hall, Manly Palmer. 1928. "The Secret Teachings of All Ages." Los Angeles: Philosophical Research Society.

Hamblin, Michael R. 2017. "Photobiomodulation and Infrared Light Therapy." Harvard Medical School.

Hawking, Stephen. 1988. "A Brief History of Time: From the Big Bang to Black Holes." New York: Bantam Books.

Hawkins, David R. 2002. "Power vs. Force: The Hidden Determinants of Human Behavior." Carlsbad, CA: Hay House.

Heidegger, Martin. 1962. "Being and Time." Translated by John Macquarrie and Edward Robinson. New York: Harper & Row.

Hinton, Geoffrey, Yoshua Bengio, and Yann LeCun. 2015. "Deep Learning." Nature 521 (7553): 436–444.

Hof, Wim. 2020. "The Wim Hof Method: Activate Your Full Human Potential." Boulder, CO: Sounds True.

Huberman, Andrew. 2023. "Neuroscience Foundations for Optimizing Sleep, Focus, and Productivity." Stanford University Digital Lectures.

Hyman, Mark. 2018. "Food: What the Heck Should I Eat?" New York: Little, Brown Spark.

Jung, Carl Gustav. 1964. "Man and His Symbols." New York: Doubleday.

Kaku, Michio. 2011. "Physics of the Future: How Science Will Shape Human Destiny and Our Daily Lives by the Year 2100." New York: Doubleday.

Kastrup, Bernardo. 2019. "The Idea of the World: A Multi-Disciplinary Argument for the Mental Nature of Reality." Winchester, UK: Iff Books.

Kruse, Jack. n.d. "Selected Articles and Research on Longevity and Light." Retrieved from https://jackkruse.com

Lipton, Bruce H. 2005. "The Biology of Belief: Unleashing the Power of Consciousness, Matter & Miracles." Carlsbad, CA: Hay House.

Milgram, Stanley. 1974. "Obedience to Authority: An Experimental View." New York: Harper & Row.

Murphy, Joseph. 1963. "The Power of Your Subconscious Mind." Englewood Cliffs, NJ: Prentice Hall.

Nestor, James. 2020. "Breath: The New Science of a Lost Art." New York: Riverhead Books.

Newberg, Andrew, and Mark Robert Waldman. 2006. "Why We Believe What We Believe: Uncovering Our Biological Need for Meaning, Spirituality, and Truth." New York: Free Press.

Penrose, Roger. 1989. "The Emperor's New Mind: Concerning Computers, Minds, and the Laws of Physics." Oxford: Oxford University Press.

Perlmutter, David. 2013. "Grain Brain: The Surprising Truth about Wheat, Carbs, and Sugar—Your Brain's Silent Killers." New York: Little, Brown Spark.

Rand, William Lee. 2000. "Reiki: The Healing Touch." International Center for Reiki Training.

Raz, Amir. 2007. "Hypnosis and the Brain: State of the Art." American Journal of Clinical Hypnosis 49 (4): 315–330.

Sheldrake, Rupert. 2012. "The Science Delusion: Freeing the Spirit of Enquiry." London: Coronet.

Sinclair, David A. 2019. "Lifespan: Why We Age—and Why We Don't Have To." New York: Atria Books.

Sinek, Simon. 2009. "Start With Why: How Great Leaders Inspire Everyone to Take Action." New York: Portfolio.

Tolle, Eckhart. 1997. "The Power of Now: A Guide to Spiritual Enlightenment." Novato, CA: New World Library.

Thoreau, Henry David. 1854. "Walden; or, Life in the Woods." Boston: Ticknor and Fields.

Varela, Francisco J., Evan Thompson, and Eleanor Rosch. 1991. "The Embodied Mind: Cognitive Science and Human Experience." Cambridge, MA: MIT Press.

Walker, Norman W. 1978. "Fresh Vegetable and Fruit Juices." Norwalk Press.

Weil, Andrew. 2004. "Integrative Medicine and Herbal Remedies." University of Arizona Center for Integrative Medicine.

Wilber, Ken. 2000. "A Theory of Everything: An Integral Vision for Business, Politics, Science, and Spirituality." Boston: Shambhala.

Williams, David G. 2005. "Health & Healing Newsletter: Oxygen Therapies and Hydrogen Peroxide." Mountain Home Publishing.

Willett, Walter. 2017. "Eat, Drink, and Be Healthy: The Harvard Medical School Guide to Healthy Eating." New York: Free Press.

Zohar, Danah, and Ian Marshall. 2000. "SQ: Connecting with Our Spiritual Intelligence." New York: Bloomsbury.

www.ingramcontent.com/pod-product-compliance
Lightning Source LLC
Chambersburg PA
CBHW060320050426
42449CB00011B/2580